THINK
L I K E   A
HACKER
A Sysadmin's Guide to Cybersecurity

by
Michael J. Melone

Disclaimer

This book was prepared by Michael J. Melone in his personal capacity. The opinions expressed in this book are the author's own and do not necessarily reflect the views of his employer, Microsoft.

"The difference between a ½" book and a 1 ½" book is 1" of bullshit"

– James Whittaker
@DocJamesW

Contents

Prologue

Information security has become one of the most rapidly changing and advancing fields within information technology, in large part due to targeted attacks. As we become a more connected society, hackers become more connected to our confidential information, financial institutions, and other sensitive systems.

Why is it that we can't seem to keep these attackers out of our networks? Many organizations spend millions of dollars annually in software licenses, employee salaries, and consulting fees to limit the likelihood that their organization is compromised next – yet they continue to be compromised.

Today's compromises easily circumvent protections which were implemented to defend networks prior to the advent of targeted attacks. Targeted attack became relevant in 2005 when the world was introduced to Stuxnet. Touted as the first "weapons grade" malware, Stuxnet was the first known malware that transcended a cyber-attack into the physical world. Since then, the world has been introduced to numerous variants of remote access Trojans, ransomware, wipers, credential theft tools, and various other forms of malware which enable an attacker to rapidly take control of and impact a target network.

As software developers know, vulnerability is preventable yet inevitable. While our understanding of secure software development improves, so do our processes for developing such software, resulting in finished products of higher quality. Professionally-trained software developers undergo rigorous training regarding the risks associated with buffer overflows, integer underflows, injection attacks, and the numerous other forms of software vulnerabilities which can be exploited to enable execution of arbitrary code.

Improvements in secure software development have led to software manufacturers incorporating regular updating as part of their software package, reduced number of zero-day software vulnerabilities (those that the manufacturer has not yet patched), and a reduction in the overall number of critical vulnerabilities throughout the world. Despite these improvements, we've seen an alarming increase in the number of networks compromised by attackers worldwide. Why is that?

1

Hackers have found another form of vulnerability which runs unbridled throughout most enterprises. This class of vulnerability isn't typically monitored and managed by the security development lifecycle (SDL), though it should be. These vulnerabilities reside in system design rather than software design, and they're largely responsible for enabling hackers to rapidly translate a single compromised host into compromise of an entire enterprise.

Cybersecurity is SDL for the systems engineers of the world. Hackers have learned that egregious delegation of administration runs rampant throughout enterprises. Hackers have also reaffirmed that humans remain vulnerable regardless of the amount of training they are provided. If hackers can get one user to launch their malcode, the entire enterprise can fall.

In this book, we will discuss the cybersecurity problem space, examine how a hacker looks at a target network, and theorize on how to remediate and prevent compromise in the future. We will work together to train your mind to see your enterprise through the eyes of a hacker – as a series of access points and forms of authorization. Together, we will review the benefits and drawbacks behind authentication and authorization design and discuss how we can improve information security during the design phase, rather than trying to patch vulnerabilities in a production system after the fact. Let's take a journey together and learn how to think like a hacker.

What is Cybersecurity?

Cybersecurity is a newer term in information security, but it tends to be met with some confusion. What is it that differentiates a cybersecurity professional from other forms of information security professionals? Some feel it is a more elevated position in the field, others feel it is more of a technical approach, and still others think it is just another term for the same skill set or expertise. To begin, I will attempt to define the unique characteristics of a cybersecurity professional that cause them to differ from those focused on other aspects of information security, such as compliance, legal, or operational security.

The cybersecurity realm of information security was born from the increase in targeted attacks. Prior to determined human adversary (DHA) activity (hacking performed by well-funded and organized hacking groups), there was little thought given to hacking into enterprise networks outside of national defense and government organizations. The increased prevalence and impact of cyber-attacks occurring in private sector organizations gave birth to the need for a type of cybersecurity professional who understood not only how something could be used, but also how it could be abused using hacking tools or methodology.

Cybersecurity is a technical branch of information security with a heavy focus on wargaming (an exercise performed by an individual or organization in an attempt to find hidden vulnerabilities through thought experiments and testing). This field of information security is like penetration testing, but tends to have a more defensive approach. Cybersecurity professionals typically take a white-box approach to analysis (i.e., the configuration and layout of the enterprise are available and commonly the basis for analysis) and attempt to find ways to obtain and increase their abilities within an organization.

Cybersecurity professionals take an "assume breach" mentality when assessing an organization. This mindset tends to be different from traditional information security whereby significant investment is made to prevent the initial breach from occurring. In today's environment, most enterprises are expansive and contain a seemingly infinite number of entry points that are exploitable by a hacker. With this level of complexity, it becomes likely that an attacker will be able to find one or more entryways

3

into the enterprise. For this reason, cybersecurity professionals tend to focus more on what an attacker can do once he or she obtains initial access. Additionally, they focus on potential vulnerabilities within the organization which provide significant (i.e., administrative) authority within the enterprise. The more value that an asset would have to a hacker, the more closely the cybersecurity professional will focus on its analysis.

Malicious Individuals vs. Malicious Software

Another key characteristic of cybersecurity professionals is the understanding that the targets they are hunting are not traditional malware. Before the rise of cybersecurity, most malicious activity was associated with malware – software whose intent and capabilities were largely written into the code itself. This malware would operate autonomously and steal valuable information, perform destructive activities, or generally wreak mayhem completely autonomously through instructions embedded within its code.

Cybersecurity professionals deal with a very different type of threat – one typically controlled by humans. Dealing with a DHA threat means these professionals are fighting someone, not something, and requires a different approach than battling a piece of software that takes over an enterprise.

Unlike traditional malware, DHA organizations will change strategies periodically. These strategic changes can be due to several factors that include, but are not limited to, the following:

- Different attackers controlling the malware
- Response to detection (commonly referred to as "tipping your hand")
- New generations of tooling or implants
- New motives

DHA attackers typically define a demarcation point between what should be automated (i.e. routine tasks performed as a normal course of action) and what should remain up for interpretation by the hacker. Automation in the DHA world is a double-edged sword. On one side, it provides fast, repeatable, and proven methods for data gathering, exploitation, etc. On the other side, highly repeatable activities are subject to signature by an antimalware product. Therefore, they run the risk of being detected and losing stealth.

Another difference when dealing with DHAs is the potential for a complete change of motive or activity, such as the following:

- An attacker who is interested in gathering intellectual property going dormant because they are waiting for something to trigger data gathering, such as a press release or a calendar schedule
- An attacker becoming destructive due to being discovered
- An attacker changing or adding implant techniques because many credentials or implants suddenly go offline

These changes in motives and activity are likely to occur without the target knowing they are going to occur.

Last, it is important to realize that the attacker may have as much (or more) access to the target than the most senior administrators of the organization. Additionally, these actors will vary in skill level and may be more knowledgeable about a service in an enterprise than the administrators. These attackers also may have access to malicious tools which can perform actions on these services that are not possible using legitimate capabilities of the service.

Access and Authorization

A cyber-attack occurs because the attackers are attempting to establish either access or authorization that they do not currently possess. Access is the ability to interface with a target, and can come in many forms. For example, a computer can be accessed physically

- By using the keyboard
- By physically removing the hard drive
- Through a variety of point-to-point mediums such as Bluetooth, USB, or a barcode scanner
- Through a networked connection intercepting an outbound network connection from the computer
- Through connecting to a hosted server service on the computer.

The concept of access is not limited to computers – a person who can call another person on the phone or can send them an email is essentially "accessing" that person, a person who can physically touch a padlock is accessing the padlock, and someone who can touch a circuit breaker panel can access all the circuit breakers within it, if it is not locked.

Authorization is the ability to perform the desired action. Just like access, authorization can be performed on anything. Many things in the world provide authorization of use to anyone who can physically access them, such as the ability to turn on or off a water faucet. When limiting authorization, typically some form of credential is used to identify the potential user, such as a key, password, or identification card issued from a trusted source. However, authorization can be tampered with - if the attacker is aware of a flaw in the target's authorization decision process. For example, an improperly coded software package is subject to exploitation, which may allow the attacker to perform activities that legitimate authorization may not permit.

Exploitation is not limited to computers, either. One great example of exploitation outside of the computer world is social engineering, where an attacker tricks a target into trusting him or her without having proper credentials. Another form of exploitation is lock picking, whereby a lock's tumblers are manipulated using a set of lock picks to emulate use of a legitimate key.

The process of attaining access and authorization typically repeats until the attacker attains the necessary level to fulfill their current strategy. Any newly-attained access and authorization could be either new or redundant. New access and authorization enables the attackers to perform more actions than before, whereas redundant access or authorization provides resiliency if an existing method of access or authorization is eliminated.

Hacker Strategy

Hackers tend 'to have specific goals or motivations in mind when performing computer hacking. Unlike most traditional malware, these goals are typically not resident in the tools discovered by incident response teams or security researchers. To facilitate organization, we will break these goals into tactical and strategic goals based on their strategic distance.

Tactical Goals

A tactical goal is one that resolves an immediate need. These goals are very short-term and typically much more technical than operational goals. Tactical goals are resolved through specific attacks. For the purposes of comparison, a tactical goal is like a single battle in a war.

Skilled hackers seeking to address tactical goals will perform different forms of profiling techniques, such as port scanning an organization's public IP space; researching organization design, reporting structure, and key individuals using social networking; or performing other forms of research to find potentially exploitable targets that they can access. Once an appropriate (and assumed vulnerable) target is identified, the attack is crafted and delivered.

The attacker does not usually care about the target itself when satisfying a tactical goal; rather, it is part of a bigger plan to accomplish a goal. Some examples of tactical goals include the following:

- Obtaining access to an unreachable asset
- Obtaining new or additional authorization to an asset

- Establishing redundant forms of persistence if one is eliminated

Strategic Goals

A strategic goal takes a more long-term vision of the cyberattack. Strategic goals are the reason that tactical operations occur – they are the "big picture" view that creates one or more individual attacks. Understanding the operational goal of an attacker reveals the ultimate goal for a given operation.

The important part to note about strategic goals is that they are not technology-related, thus removing the ability to completely combat the situation solely by focusing on removing the detected malware implants. Addressing strategic goals requires knowledge of what is of value to the attacker(s) as well as what is of value to your organization and establishing a necessary defensive strategy centered around those assets.

There are many different possible operational goals an attacker may have. Some examples of common strategic goals include the following:

Defamation

Attackers interested in defaming their target may seek to perform activities such as website defacement, theft of sensitive information, or covert monitoring of activities over time while waiting for the right opportunity to attack. Additionally, attackers interested in defamation may be interested in social networking credentials to enable them to post as the target.

Defamation attacks can be devastating when executed correctly, and are especially effective when the target is one that is assumed to be secure by the public. For example, the hacking group Anonymous occasionally tampers with public websites of prominent government organizations in order to display power. Even though compromise of a website does not directly imply compromise of the target's sensitive information systems, the public sees the tampered site and assumes that the organization is compromised.

One famous example of defamation is the alleged hacking of 2016 presidential candidate Hillary Clinton. In this example, leak of damaging information from private systems publicly discredited Clinton and were believed to be one of the reasons for her loss.

Strategic Advantage

Attackers seeking strategic advantage may be interested in research and development, pricing and other financial information, or any other information which may provide a competitive advantage over their target.

One common example of hacking for strategic advantage is intellectual property theft, or espoinage. In these attacks, highly valuable information is stolen from the target and used to avert expensive research and development costs. Once stolen, the attacker can produce cutting-edge technology with only limited investment in research and development.

Another type of strategic advantage is government intelligence gathering or interception, whereby attackers attempt to deduce future operations and activities planned by their target to establish strategic advantage in war or politics. Public examples of this motive are typically rare due to their sensitivity, but include the 2015 hack of the Office of Personnel Management (OPM) which leaked sensitive information on approximately 22 million U.S. workers holding a government security clearance.

Monetary

Many attackers simply seek monetary gain, whether direct or indirect. Attackers seeking direct monetary gain often target users in financial roles at organizations. Typically, these hackers will utilize techniques such as phishing (use of malicious email communication to socially engineer credentials from users or trick them into executing malicious code) to gain credentials to sensitive accounts used in finance.

A common example of attackers seeking direct monetary gain from hacking includes Nigerian 419 scammers, who trick targets into providing sensitive banking information. A more advanced example of this is performed by attackers who set up fake email logon pages and scam users into "logging in." Once credentials are stolen, the attackers can use the legitimate account to steal funds or to improve influence over another target to do so (i.e., if the email to the CFO asking to transfer funds is sourced from the CEO's actual mailbox, it is much more trustworthy than a fake public address seeking to do the same).

Another example of direct monetary gain involves compromise of sensitive systems which maintain sensitive financial information, such as credit card numbers. Once stolen, this information can be used for direct financial gain (using the account itself), or indirectly through sale on the black market or dark web (an anonymized subnetwork of the Internet).

Indirect monetary gain can also occur with valuable assets which are not financial in nature. For example, covertly stolen account credentials may be sold on the dark web. Other valuable assets that are bought and sold include source code, intellectual property, and identities.

Destructive

In some cases, the motivation behind activity is destructive in nature, whether for vengeance or as part of a military operation. When executed properly, a destructive attack is quick and devastating. Typically, these attacks focus on deploying malicious software designed to wipe the drives wherever they are executed. Deployment may utilize software distribution systems, systems administration tools (such as PSExec), directory services, scheduled tasks, or several other means.

One notable example of a destructive military motive is Stuxnet, the malware that impacted Iranian nuclear refinement research. In this incident, hackers obtained access to highly sensitive systems involved with enrichment of uranium, allegedly for making nuclear weaponry. Once infected, the malware was specially coded to modify operation of centrifuges to destroy them without alerting scientists operating the devices.

Hacking

At a high level, hacking is the cyclical process of establishing new access and authorization until a necessary level has been attained to carry out the intended strategic goal. Hackers seek to continually increase access and authorization throughout a target's network (tactical goals) until sufficiently positioned to execute their overall plan (strategic goal).

Defending against hackers means understanding the many avenues that they can use to enter an enterprise, maintain access, increase authorization, and execute their plans. Without a thorough understanding of how a hacker's mind works, a target is defenseless against the attack.

In the coming chapters, we will discuss the core concepts behind how a hacker works, how to remediate a network after a targeted attack, and how to defend a modern enterprise against today's hackers.

Access and Authorization

As we discussed in the previous chapter, all hacking can be distilled to the repeating search for and attainment of new access and authorization. In this chapter, we will dive deeper into the concepts of access and authorization and into the different means of attaining each.

Access

At its core, access is the ability to interface with something or someone. Access comes in many different forms – and many of them have nothing to do with computers. Access types are defined by the capabilities of the target and range significantly from the most common and obvious to the covert, obscure, and malicious.

To begin, let us look at some of the available forms of access provided by a normal computer:

- Network interfaces, which enable software running on the computer to be accessible
- Keyboard, mouse, or other input device
- Bluetooth, wireless input devices, or other forms of wireless connectivity
- Input ports, such as USB, Firewire, Thunderbolt, and HDMI
- Sensors, such as GPS, cameras, and fingerprint scanners
- Visual monitoring of displays, typing, or status indicators (surveillance only)
- Emanation, also known as EMSEC or Tempest (surveillance only)

A normal computer provides a wide array of means for access, many of which enable interactivity. The important thing to note from this thought experiment is that there are very many opportunities for a hacker to access an individual computer directly. Depending on the software running on the computer, these forms of access can provide a hacker the ability to perform profiling or intelligence gathering, execute legitimate code, or in some cases execute arbitrary code.

As previously mentioned, access is not limited to technology. If attackers can touch their target, they can perform a wide range of attacks enabled by having physical access. If the target trusts GPS navigation for reliable operation and the attackers can spoof the GPS signal, they are in effect accessing the target. Attackers able to call or send an email to a user inside of the target organization are, in effect, accessing that user and can attempt to manipulate him or her to perform activities on their behalf.

Proxy Access

Access does not need to be direct to be effective. In fact, in many cases indirect or "proxy" access can be more effective than attempting to gain physical or network access to a computer which may be behind multiple security devices.

Proxy access leverages one asset's legitimate access in order to provide access to a target on behalf of the hacker. One great example of proxy access which is commonly used is social engineering. When social engineering is performed, a hacker will coerce a target into performing an action for them, typically through some form of deception.

For example, the Stuxnet malware was designed to propagate using USB drives. The attack group relied on the common practice of people plugging in a USB drive to provide access to a likely highly secure network. Once a user inserted the infected drive into a computer, the malware loaded and infected the target.

Maintaining Access

Once new access is established, it must be made somewhat durable to remain useful. While momentary access can provide significant benefits, the ability to leverage one form of access to establish further and more durable access or authorization is more valuable. For example, a single social engineering success is useful in gaining new access to a target, but is likely not the means that the attacker will choose to perform ongoing activity.

Maintaining access to a target is typically accomplished with some form of "back door" into the organization. This back door is often a malicious reverse shell, commonly referred to as an implant or Trojan backdoor, named after the famous Trojan Horse used by the Greeks to invade the city of Troy. Software implants are ideal for an attacker for many reasons:

- Software implants typically perform an outbound connection to the attacker's server over a standard port such as TCP 80 or 443 (an activity that is rarely blocked)
- Software implants provide a basic toolkit for the attackers which usually enables them to upload and download files at will, perform

some basic reconnaissance and various forms of credential theft or attacks
- Software implants provide some level of authorization – either the user contexts they are running as (if a user implant) or the computer's system account (if a system implant)
- Software implants can be difficult to find without use of specialized tools

Other possibilities for establishing durable access include performing a configuration change, such as enabling remote desktop protocol on a server, enabling some form of VPN, or enabling legitimate management applications to pass through a firewall.

Authorization

Authorization is the ability to perform an action on a target and can be classified as either legitimate illegitimate.

Legitimate authorization is normally derived from some form of authentication from a trusted authentication source. The following are typical examples:

- Possession of a key grants legitimate access to any lock with which it is paired
- A user account is granted authorization to resources required for its proper use
- Anyone in possession of the security code for a gate is authorized to open the gate
- A manager is authorized to give direction to his or her subordinates

It is important to delineate that legitimate authorization comes from the perspective of the authorization, not necessarily the context it is used.

- If someone were to steal the key, he or she could illegitimately open the lock; however, from the lock's perspective the authorization was legitimate
- A stolen user account could be used to perform malicious activity; however, from the perspective of the server infrastructure the user was legitimately authorized to perform the actions
- A person can provide other unauthorized individuals with the code to the security gate – from the perspective of the gate, the user is authorized because he or she provided the correct code
- A person can research information about the target organization and masquerade as a senior executive on a phone call and reset the

employee's password. If proper protocol was followed, the user performing the password reset acted legitimately

Illegitimate authorization leverages flaws in design, software vulnerabilities, or other security error to perform an activity. The line that separates legitimate from illegitimate authorization is the error aspect: the authorization was an unintended consequence of a flaw or limitation. Some examples of illegitimate authorization include the following:

- Utilizing a set of lock picks to open a lock for which the attacker does not have the key
- Tricking users into performing unauthorized activity over a phone call by placing them in a high-stress situation
- Exploiting a vulnerability in a software package that grants the attacker additional unintended authorization
- Using debug access to an operating system to read credentials from other user sessions

In each of the above cases, the attacker used a vulnerable circumstance surrounding the security control to provide unintended additional authorization.

Authentication

Authentication is the process of establishing some form of identity to which we can attribute authorization. Authentication can come from several sources:

- An ID card issued from a trusted source (a company-issued ID, federally-issued ID, passport, etc.)
- Physical possession of a key (in the case of a lock)
- Knowledge of a shared secret for a given account
- A key pair sharing a form of asymmetric security association

Authentication will be covered more in-depth in a later chapter. For the purposes of this section, it is important to identify that authentication and authorization are two separate concepts – authentication being the establishment of an identity and authorization being the list of activities that an identified entity can perform.

Excessive Authorization

One of the common issues with authorization is that it is typically granted too broadly. In many cases, general groups of access control entries are allotted to an identity to simplify manageability. Unfortunately, this excessive authorization means that users can perform significantly more activities than are likely necessary, which poses unnecessary risk when dealing with malicious activity.

A physical world equivalent to this would be using a single key to open most of the locks required by a user in the organization. Although efficient, maintaining this state means that the key would likely need to open many more locks than would be necessary for every user to perform. More specifically, imagine if every door had a "default lock" which corresponded to that same key and needed to be manually changed to prevent access. This is the condition created by the "domain users" and "domain admins" groups in Active Directory.

Another source of excessive authorization stems from users who reside within an organization for a longer period and change roles during their tenure. This condition, sometimes referred to as "authorization creep," may result in disproportionately powerful users simply because they continually gain additional authorization as they change roles.

Imagine people who are issued a new key with every role that they undertake at an organization, while previous keys are not taken from them when they leave their former role. In this condition, they would still be able to access all locks that their previous roles provided them access to, in addition to all the locks that their current role allows them to access. In this condition, their keyring would be disproportionately more valuable than anyone else in their role.

Proxy Authorization

Another means of establishing authorization is proxy authorization, or using another asset with legitimate authority to perform an action on behalf of an unauthorized user. In the physical world, proxy authorization could mean convincing a person who legitimately has a key to a door to open the door for someone who lacks access and let him or her in – or sneaking in behind people with access because they did not check to ensure the door closed behind them. In this condition, one could obtain access to any door that the keyholder had access to if one is able to successfully execute the maneuver.

A common example of proxy authorization is software exploitation, whereby attackers identify a logic flaw in an application which enables them to cause the application to perform an action on their behalf using the authorization imparted to that application. For example, if attackers find an application which is vulnerable to SQL injection, they will be able to perform any activity that the identity of the SQL server account can perform. If that SQL server utilizes a domain account with sufficient access and authorization, then the attackers may not need to perform any additional work to accomplish their mission.

A similar form of exploitation may be used to obtain access beyond the identity of the application. These exploits, known as elevation of privilege attacks, can be used to increase the authorization of executed code by exploiting a vulnerability in more privileged libraries used to support the application, such as operating system modules or common language runtime executables. In this condition, a successful attack may yield access up to the available authorization of the vulnerable module. If the vulnerability is in an operating system executable, the attacker may be able to perform any activity that the operating system could.

Credential Theft

One of the more common means of obtaining authorization is through some form of credential theft. Returning to our previous example of the person who has a physical key to a door, credential theft would be the equivalent of obtaining that person's key and making a copy of it for your own use. This key would remain valid if the lock did not change and would provide access to every lock which paired with that key.

Credential theft comes in many different implementations, but many of them can be distilled down to a small handful of novel techniques. This book is not intending to cover every known technique or implementation used to perform credential theft, but rather will focus on the core concepts of the most frequently used techniques. Additionally, defenses against credential theft will be covered in a later chapter.

Keylogging

The easiest and most direct way to perform credential theft is through keylogging. A keylogger will monitor any keys typed by the user and record them to a file for later analysis, or may periodically send the recorded keystrokes to a remote server. Keyloggers come in many forms that range from covert software to devices that intercept the connection between the keyboard and the computer to entire keyboard replacements. In some cases, such as with ATMs, keylogging is performed using a covert camera with view of the PIN pad.

Monitoring

Monitoring attacks works by surveilling a target and waiting for authentication to occur. These attacks require the attacker to have preexisting access to the communication channel where authentication will occur. Additionally, the communication must be unprotected or previously circumvented for the attacker to have sufficient access to perform this attack (I.e., a stolen session encryption key, a shared secret, or a Wi-Fi network credential, when encryption is employed).

In a monitoring attack, the attacker watches traffic and waits for an unprotected authentication to occur. When this occurs, the credential is harvested from the session and used to provide access and / or authorization to the service.

Man-in-the-Middle

A man-in-the-middle attack occurs when the attacker intercepts traffic between a target's system and a server. To execute this attack, the target must be tricked to connect to the attacker's system, which subsequently relays the connection to the legitimate server. In many cases, this technique is performed to circumvent asymmetric encryption capabilities, commonly SSL. Once intercepted, the attacker can view and modify any traffic sent between the systems, and thus can obtain unprotected credentials.

A typical man-in-the-middle attack begins by tampering with name resolution (the means that a computer uses to establish the IP address of a server from a more human-readable name) or routing (controlling how traffic flows over a network to route some or all of it through an attacker-controlled device). Once attackers can control one of these aspects of communication, they can selectively intercept the traffic and utilize a fake certificate to trick the user into thinking he or she is connecting to a valid server. Once connected, the attackers can then create a connection to the real server and route all traffic through their computer. Data encrypted by the target will utilize the fake key provided by the attackers, which they can then decrypt, log, and relay to the actual server. It is worth noting that in many of these cases the user will be prompted with a certificate warning because the attacker-issued certificate usually is not from a trusted source.

Pass the Hash

Another common technique used for credential theft is pass the hash – a technique that leverages preexisting access paired with local administrator authorization to read protected system memory and extract authentication credentials directly from memory. This attack works against any form of single sign-on authentication and affects any operating system which provides an interface allowing administrators to read memory where credentials are stored for authentication.

Pass the hash is a very powerful capability for a hacker and is typically employed in one of two ways.

First, an attacker may use a pass the hash utility to monitor credentials used on a compromised machine. These credentials include all interactive sessions on the machine, which may include highly valuable administrative credentials. Attackers have been known to intentionally break some aspect of the computer to cause a PC technician to log on, thus exposing the technician's credentials to theft.

The second method, known as lateral traversal, uses an existing credential's authorization to attack other assets at its same level. Lateral traversal enables an attacker to use a stolen credential to infect several machines, increasing the likelihood of capturing an administrator credential.

Social Engineering - Hacking Humans

Social engineering is the general term used to describe the act of performing psychological manipulation to get a target to perform a desired action. Humans are an ideal target for a hacker for many reasons:

- They likely already have access and authorization within the target organization
- People are susceptible to manipulation due to cognitive biases
- Employees of the organization are typically easy to reach externally through different means (I.e., phone, text messages, e-mail, etc.)
- Social engineering, with appropriate profiling, can be used to get the attackers very close to their target of interest

The following sections describe different forms of social engineering and provide context on how they work.

Phishing

One of the most common means of social engineering is phishing: sending enticing communications with the intention of tricking users into performing actions or leaking sensitive data, typically over email. Some examples of common commodity phishing emails include the fake prince who needs to transfer money, fake lottery winning notifications, malware masquerading as fake shipment notifications, and fake security notifications from banks or other public websites.

A subcategory of phishing, called spear phishing, refers to when an attacker personalizes the communication to the target to increase the likelihood that he or she will perform the intended action. Spear phishing attempts may use public company information or documents which are commonly renamed with alluring titles, or they may speak directly to the user's interests by harvesting information from social media, news, or other sources. Attackers will typically send malicious resumes, fake corporate strategy documents, or links to a legitimate-looking login page for webmail or company portal.

Phone Call

Social engineering with a phone call is another very common way to manipulate a user. Common examples of non-targeted social engineering over the phone include the infamous fake calls from Microsoft about computer problems, fake IRS calls, and fake bank calls.

Typically, the goal is to establish either a sense of familiarity or a sense of urgency which causes the targets to bypass their logic and resolve the situation as quickly as possible. Targeted social engineering calls typically include some form of research, such as identifying senior people inside the organization to increase the apparent validity of the call. Anyone interested in seeing this in action should attend the "social engineering village" at a DEFCON conference to see how simply this can be achieved.

Baiting

Baiting is a very powerful social engineering tool where the attacker leaves a device such as a USB memory stick in an area where members of the target organization are likely to be. In some cases, this device may contain the organization's logo or an alluring label such as "confidential" or "salary information" to increase the likelihood that a target will plug it in.

Once plugged in, many computers may attempt to automatically launch a predefined file on the drive which causes the installation of a remote access Trojan or another malware. In other cases, a compromised productivity document may be placed at the root of the drive in hopes that the target will open it, thereby infecting the computer. Another approach is for the hardware itself to be malicious through use of specialized firmware and drivers.

One famous case of this approach occurred in 2008 when the market was saturated with malicious digital photo frames. Once plugged in to a target's USB port, these photo frames would infect the host with the mocmex Trojan. Once infected, mocmex would collect sensitive information from infected machines and forward it to attacker-controlled servers.

Vulnerability Chaining

Significant compromises are the result of multiple breaches in security – an iterative process whereby the attacker continually gains new and differing forms of access and authorization until the appropriate context is obtained. Each of these individual breaches make up a link within a chain of events, ultimately leading to the compromise that provides the attacker the necessary access and authorization.

To perform vulnerability chain analysis, it is important to have a solid understanding of the individual pieces involved in the chain. The following sections will cover each piece separately, ultimately culminating in an explanation of its implementation.

Securable

A securable is anything that can have a control applied which restricts its use or operation to a subset of identities. The ability to control access is important, since an asset without the ability to control authorization either allows anything or nothing to interact with it, thus eliminating the need to assess its security.

Securables typically allow for flexibility in how they provide authorization: for example, one identity might have read access to a file, whereas another may be able to write to it. Authorization may also be granted at the operating system level, such as how backup software enables the reading of any file controlled by the operating system. In the computer world, these different lists of identities and authorization assignments are typically referred to as an access control list.

In the physical world, a securable could be considered a lock – such as the one on a post office box. Users might have a key that allows them to access their personal post office box, but would not necessarily allow them to open the one next to theirs. On the other hand, mail workers likely possess a key to a lock that will enable them to access any of the post office boxes in order to perform mail delivery.

Principal

For the concept of authorization to exist, there must be some form of principal (a.k.a security principal). A principal is anything granting authorization – such as a user credential, a key, a physical badge, or a credential. In the software world, principals are commonly user accounts.

A principal is the identity which you are trying to prove using some form of authentication. It is the user, the service, or entity – the "noun" if you will – that you are identifying and providing authorization. Possession of a validated identity as a principal enables authorization to everything that principal is permitted.

Membership

One identity can represent multiple principals as is common through group membership. Membership is a concept whereby one principal can act on behalf of another due to association. This association makes assigning and maintaining authorization easier because in many cases more than a single entity must be assigned a given form of authorization. Additionally, this ensures consistent authorization is provided to principals acting in the same capacity.

Membership enables a set of authorizations and/or a set of principals to be grouped together. These groupings are typically used to define the accesses associated with a specific role – such as all accesses required for a backup service, or accesses required for a person to perform as a help desk technician or systems administrator.

A physical world example would be a keyring with multiple keys: whoever has the keyring can open any lock that corresponds with one of the keys on the ring.

Authenticator

An authenticator Is a credential used to prove the identity of a principal, such as a password or an ID card. Authenticators must undergo validation to ensure that they belong to the principal which they are identifying; however, the level of validation varies based on the authenticator provided.

Some authenticators are simple, such as a password or the possession of a physical card. Other authenticators may require multiple factors to sufficiently prove the identity of the principal, and the number and types of these factors may differ based on the authenticating entity or the context of the authentication (some forms of authorization may be more sensitive than others and thus may require additional proof of authenticity).

Factors used in authentication vary widely based on the type of authentication being performed and may include one or more of the following:

- Knowledge of a shared secret
- Proof of possession of the corresponding key in a key pair
- Photographic validation
- Biometric authentication (fingerprint, retina, vein pattern, etc.)
- Possession of a physical entity, such as a key

The above list is very short compared to the number of different factors which can be used to prove an identity to an authenticating entity.

Trust

Trust is a concept which exists when the authenticating entity does not itself issue the identities which it uses to provide authorization to securables. Trust may be direct or indirect. A direct trust means that the authenticating entity is one degree of separation away from the entity which issued the identity. Indirect trust, on the other hand, means that the identity is trusted by an entity which the authenticating entity trusts, but the authenticating entity is not directly trusted.

One physical world example of trust is state-issued identity cards. The identity card issuing authority acts on behalf of the state and creates ID cards. Any state governmental body (and virtually every organization in the state) trusts these identity cards because they trust the issuing body which created the card – this would be a direct trust. Additionally, that ID card can be used with organizations in other states which trust the issuing state – this would be an indirect trust.

If the principal identified by the ID card were to use it in an entirely different part of the world, however, the ID card is unlikely to be trusted. In this case, a different credential which is trusted by the authenticating entity (such as a passport) must be used to prove the identity of the principal, thus granting the principal its appropriate authorization.

Domain

A domain is a term used to describe a system which either proves the identity of a principal or controls access to a securable. Domains are very important in authentication and thus must be protected. Compromise of a domain subsequently compromises the integrity of any identities issued by the domain as well as the security of any securables protected by the domain.

In the physical world, a domain might be compared to a state ID office or passport office. Organizations can trust authenticators issued from these "domains" if the ID issuance process from these entities can be trusted.

Should the ID issuance process become compromised, authenticators issued from that entity can no longer be guaranteed to be authentic.

Another example of a domain is a security guard for a building. If the security guard is trustworthy, he or she can be trusted to protect the security of assets within the building. However, if the security guard has questionable associations, his or her judgement may not be quite as trustworthy.

Standard and Administrative Authorization

Authorization to a resource can be broken down into two generic categories: standard and administrative authorization. Standard authorization is what is likely provided to most principals accessing the resource. A principal with standard authorization has some form of permission to use the resource. In short, having standard authorization to a resource cannot provide any additional authorization because of its use.

In almost every case, both principals and domains are securables as well. The securable aspect of these assets provide for administration – such as the following:

- The ability to add or remove trusts for a domain
- The ability to add, remove, or change the authenticator(s) for a principal
- The ability to add or remove principals authorized to administer the domain
- The ability to add or remove principals authorized to maintain authenticators for a principal
- The ability to add, remove, or change members of a group which controls authorization to securables
- The ability to add, remove, or change the principals allowed to override the access control list set on a securable
- The ability to read the authenticator(s) used for principals authenticated by a domain

In each of these cases, the activities described are necessary for normal operation; however, they are significantly more sensitive than standard authorization.

Administrative authorization enables the principal to assume the identity of a securable or can allow the principal to take over a securable. When a principal has administrative authorization over another principal, he or she can assume the identity of that principal and thereby gain all of the authorization that the target principal possesses. In the case where a principal has administrative authorization over a domain, that principal can masquerade as any securable controlled by that domain and impersonate any user authenticated by that domain.

Administrative authorization does not necessarily need to be an access control list entry that provides explicit authorization over a principal or domain. In some cases, assets required by a sensitive asset may be utilized to take over or provide administrative equivalent authorization to the principal or domain. For example, the ability to read a file containing a list of passwords to user accounts on the network is the equivalent to being able to take over that user account. The same condition works in the computer world: the ability to write to a file which executes on behalf of the operating system will likely provide the ability to act as the operating system, and thus is equivalent to administrative authorization.

Putting It All Together

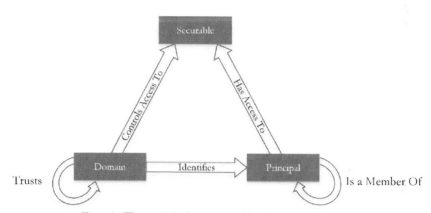

Figure 1 - The association between securables, domains, and principals

Once security is distilled into these concepts, we can start looking at models which enable analysis to:

- Find security deficiencies
- Discover highly valued principals and their associated administrative authorization
- Establish chains which we can use to improve the overall security of our operation

There are many cases whereby administrative authorization is intended; however, there are conditions where individual configurations result in much more powerful authorization than intended. This condition manifests for any of several reasons, including the following:

- Authorization creep
- Design oversight
- Test configurations
- Lack of least-privilege design
- Laziness

In these cases, there may be a path between where the attackers start and the access and authorization they require. If the path already exists, then the effort required to attain the necessary access and authorization may be shortened.

The linking together of each individual vulnerability from a starting point to the required authorization is called vulnerability chaining. Interrupting any of these chains will render the path impracticable, and thus improve security posture against the loss of that authorization.

Managing Legitimate Administrative Authorization

Due to its necessity, administrative authorization can most likely be reduced, but likely not eliminated. In these cases, the solution is to baseline the normal operation of these principals through logging and monitoring, and alerting when activity violates this baseline. Where possible, logging should be centralized such that an attacker is unable to remove evidence of malicious activity at will.

One solution to this situation is to monitor any administrative authorization used on known principals with such authorization capability. Use of such authority should be rare and limited, therefore lending itself to alerting. For example, the system could alert anytime a user who has membership in an administrative group has their password reset (i.e. changed by a principal other than itself, or without authenticating as the principal in order to perform the change). This activity could mean that an attacker who does not currently have equivalent authorization may be attempting to obtain authorization by setting the user's authenticator.

Another solution is to establish a baseline of how a given principal utilizes his or her administrative authority to determine what "normal" looks like for that principal. Once established, deviations from normal activity can be used to identify potentially malicious activity. However, it is worth noting that one must assume that the principal is not compromised when establishing what "normal" looks like for that principal – lest malicious activity become "normal" and thus never identified.

An important thing to keep in mind when establishing alerts is that limiting the number of alerts is critical for monitoring. A monitoring solution which constantly flags legitimate activity is likely to be ignored due to the overhead required to filter through the "noise" and get to events of interest. An alerting solution that generates significant noise is likely to not be used.

Examples of Vulnerability Chaining

Now that we have an idea of what vulnerability chaining is let's see how we can use it to analyze some potentially risky security configurations. Note that these only represent a few of many possible situations that may exist.

Case 1: Obtaining Access to the CEO's Mailbox

In our first case, we will assume that User 1 is a PC technician working for the targeted organization. The attacker has stolen the password of User 1 through one of several means – keylogging, discovering a password file, pass the hash, etc. User 1 is a member of a group called "PC Technicians" which can reset the password of any user account within a domain where the CEO's user account also exists. The CEO can legitimately access their mailbox.

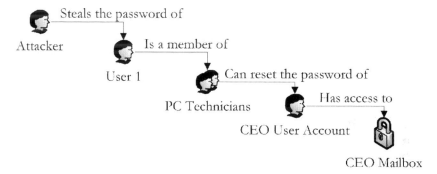

Figure 2 - Obtaining Access to the CEO's Mailbox

The situation depicted by the above diagram is very common – a group possesses blanket authority to reset passwords as part of their job. For obvious reasons, the CEO must be able to access their mailbox; thus, this is not a viable place to impart restrictions or monitoring. The administrative authority used in this chain is the reset of the CEO's password by the "PC Technicians" group – an action which should be infrequent enough to manage.

Three possible solutions exist to this situation:

- Limit the number of accounts for which the "PC Technicians" group can reset the password, such that the CEO's account is not included

- Monitor password resets performed by the "PC Technicians" group
- Monitor all password reset attempts on the CEO's user account

Each of these solutions is effective at either mitigating the vulnerability chain or monitoring its use.

Case 2: Becoming a Domain Admin

Another common goal for an attacker is to obtain a credential for, or membership in, the Active Directory group "Domain Admins." By default, these credentials have local administrator membership on every computer joined to the domain. Additionally, the domain admins group has some of the most powerful authorization within the Active Directory domain.

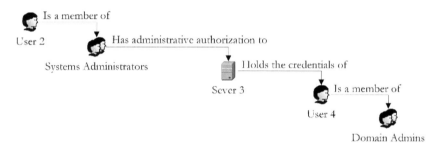

Figure 3 - Becoming a Domain Admin

In this example, User 2 is a member of a group called "systems administrators" in Active Directory. This group has administrative access to a server called "server 3." The next link in the chain is left intentionally vague – server 3 holds the credentials of "User 4" which is a member of the "Domain Admins" group. There are multiple ways that server 3 can hold the credentials of User 4, including the following:

- User 4 logged on to server 3 interactively, thus exposing a pass the hash risk
- Server 3 has a file with User 4's credentials saved on it; in which case, anyone with read access could obtain the credentials
- A key logger or other input monitoring software can be installed for cross-session use with local administrator authorization, thus capturing User 4's credentials if typed from Server 3

Here we are dealing with legitimate administrative authority on server 3, presumed to be necessary for members of the "Systems Administrators" group to do their job. There are two solutions to reduce the risk of this vector being utilized: either User 4 can be removed from the domain admins group, or User 4 can be prevented from performing interactive logon to server 3. Unfortunately, it is quite difficult to detect and prevent User 4's password from being stored in a file in a readable location to User 3.

Case 3: Social Engineering

In our third case, the attacker will use social engineering to obtain new access and authorization by manipulating a user who has local administrator authorization to his or her computer. This access will enable the attacker to install an implant that can run with privileges as high as system, and thus span user sessions or perform pass the hash attacks.

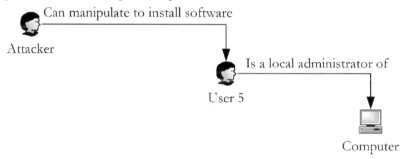

Figure 4 - Social Engineering

Presumably, it would be unethical and ineffective to monitor and control all forms of communication that "User 5" could receive: therefore, this path cannot be mitigated in that manner. Many organizations work hard to perform social engineering training for their employees, though the impact can be quite limited against a skilled attacker.

The best defense in this case is to remove "User 5" from the administrators group on his or her computer, though for many organizations this is a challenge. Unfortunately, the attackers know this and capitalize on this vulnerability to provide easy entry to an organization.

Implementing Security Controls and Monitoring

In each of the above examples, notice that there is at least one place where implementing either a security control or monitoring can provide great value towards improving the security posture of an organization. In many cases, these checkpoints are only easily visible once the entire chain is laid out.

There are a few aspects to notice about what type of controls should be implemented and in what way. First, notice that security controls are applied to high value principals. These high valued principals are the "crown jewel" targets for a hacker – providing additional access and authorization into the target enterprise networks.

Second, notice that monitoring was placed on specific access control types applied to high value securables. Monitoring all access to a securable, or a specific access to any securable, results in noisy and ineffective monitoring.

Third, all protections pertained to authorization, not access. In high security situations, limiting access may be a considerable solution, but in most cases the ability of a user with legitimate credentials to legitimately use a resource outweighs the value of making it inaccessible in the interest of information security. This is the wave of the future as devices become more and more connected, and as we move our workload to the cloud.

A note on the third point – this is not to say that we should completely neglect access-based protections, but rather shift their focus to system design and reduce our reliance on them. For example, there is likely little reason to leave services exposed to the Internet if they do not provide a benefit to standard usage of the service provided by that system – that would just be reckless. In contrast, the recommendation is to design the solution to limit exposure to necessary ports for functionality and to focus monitoring and detection on the use of authorization. This concept will be covered in additional detail in a later chapter.

Backdoors and Implants

Typically, one of the first activities that attackers will perform once they gain access and authorization to a target machine is to install some form of implant. Implants are utilized by an attacker to provide durable access and authorization within the target environment. Access is typically provided over an existing publicly-accessible network port for inbound access (such as a malicious web page on a web server), or through an outbound connection which utilizes common network ports, such as TCP 80 or TCP 443, to connect to an attacker-controlled server (commonly a reverse shell).

Implants also provide some form of authorization to the target based on the context in which they are launched. For example, an implant that launches as a user can perform any actions that the user's principal is authorized to perform. Implants launched in the system's context provides system-level authorization, thus enabling them to perform any activity possible in the context of that computer.

Also, the implant may include an advanced toolkit to enable the attacker to carry out a range of attacks without needing to download separate toolkits or applications.

Anatomy of an Implant

All implants have certain attributes and capabilities which make them useful to an attacker. In this section, we will cover these requirements and provide examples of different methods which may be employed to accomplish them.

Implant Code

Every implant needs some sort of code or compiled executable to operate. In many cases the code is an executable binary, though this is not always the case. Some implants utilize interpreted code or scripting engines to make their applications less easy to emulate with an antivirus engine.

The implant code defines the operation and capabilities of the implant; thus, it is typically safeguarded in one or more ways. Once a reverse engineer can decipher how an implant operates, it becomes easier to identify and eliminate programmatically.

Obfuscation

A common theme in implant development is the use of encryption, obfuscation, or other methods which cause the implant to be difficult to analyze. Basic obfuscation is available for many languages, commonly referred to as "packers." This technique is designed primarily to prevent reverse engineering of the code or emulation by an antivirus engine – whether to protect the design of a proprietary software package, or to prevent analysis of a malicious implant or tool.

Packers come in many forms, ranging from off-the-shelf free or commercial versions (some which even include a publicly available unpack function, such as UPX) to those that have proprietary implementations designed to dodge antivirus detection through obscurity.

Polymorphism

Another technique used to dodge detection is called polymorphism. A polymorphic file is one whose hash changes in some manner between installations, either by changing arbitrary data fields within the implant or simply padding it with bogus data at the end of the file. These files are designed to hinder research by information security professionals who are trying to determine if anyone has seen the file before or whether it was deemed malicious by searching for it by its hash.

Researching of a polymorphic implant requires the use of fuzzy hashing algorithms such as Context Triggered Piecewise Hash (CTPH). Unlike cryptographic hashes, fuzzy hashes are designed to collide or be very similar when the contents of two files are very similar.

Thread Injection

Some malware implants use other processes to host their malcode in order to hide their presence or obfuscate their code. Most operating systems allow for a capability called thread injection whereby a process can connect to another process in the same session, write to its memory space, and start code within it. This behavior is common and used legitimately by many applications; however, it can also be used to covertly run code without identifying the executable responsible for its creation.

If an implant utilizes thread injection for stealth reasons, it is unlikely that the originating executable will continue execution after the thread has been created in the new hosting process. Additionally, if the identity of the process which launched the malcode can debug an operating system process, the malicious thread could be created in any session and with authority of any interactively logged on user.

Rootkits and Hiding

Files associated with an implant must remain hidden in some manner to prevent them from being detected by IT professionals or information security software. One common technique used to deceive users and IT staff is for the implant to masquerade as a legitimate application, but in the wrong location. This technique can be effective in preventing human detection, but is unlikely to deceive antimalware programs (in some ways, masquerading may increase its likelihood of detection).

Hiding the implant from the user is a bit more difficult, but still simple. One typical way of hiding is by detouring, or "hooking," calls to read the file from disk. As a normal user, an attacker can only hook functions for that user's session, but not for every file within the operating system's control. On the other hand, an attacker with local administrator authorization can hide his or her file from the operating system as well as all users of the machine using a similar procedure. It is worth noting that the file can still be discovered by manually parsing data on the volume.

A third way to hide from detection is to load from an abnormal location, such as a registry key (i.e. Powessere backdoors) or WMI object (i.e. WMIGhost backdoors). This technique is somewhat more recent and capitalizes on the expectation that all malware should exist as some form of file. In addition, some attackers will store an entire (usually encoded) executable within a registry key and utilize a script to load it directly into memory without any file-based representation.

There are many more ways to hide the presence of an implant, but in the interest of concision they will not be discussed in this book.

Command and Control

Command and control refers to the connection which is used by the implant to communicate with the attacker. Maintaining the confidentiality of the command and control channel is critical to the implant – if identified, the target can easily sever attacker control.

Directionality

Although it is possible for the attacker to establish inbound connectivity, most implants perform an outbound connection to an attacker-controlled resource. Inbound connectivity tends to provide a significantly greater challenge than outbound since firewalls and other network security devices typically monitor or restrict inbound connections to most endpoints. In contrast, many security devices allow outbound connectivity, especially when connectivity is established over a common port.

Protocol

Many implants attempt to blend in with normal user traffic as much as possible to avoid detection; thus, HTTP and HTTPS are very commonly used for command and control. In most environments, it would be difficult to detect a small number of connections to an anomalous website due to the typical amount of varied web traffic produced by endpoints during normal operation. Additionally, few organizations have the resources available to take a whitelist approach and approve every website that a user can visit.

In some cases, HTTP calls can be made to legitimate websites hosting a malicious subsite or page such as a privately hosted blog. Other implants utilize user-submitted content to legitimate pages as demonstrated by the BlackCoffee malware variant which stored control information as comments on Microsoft TechNet blog pages. Some implants will even use advanced obfuscation techniques such as steganography (hiding data encoded within other files) as was demonstrated by the Gatak \ Stegoloader malware implant which sent PNG images encoded with encrypted commands.

Some implants use other protocols for command and control, such as SMTP (email), ICMP (ping), and DNS. In the interest of brevity, we will not dig into each of these implementations: they show that any network protocol can be used for command and control, especially more common ones.

Frequency and Statefulness

An implant does not necessarily need to be constantly connected to a command and control point throughout its operation. In fact, many implants work using a job queueing system where only a single call is made to the command and control point when the malware is started.

Auto Start Entry Point

For the implant to be usable it must have some means of launching. Modern operating systems have many locations where applications can be registered to allow them to start automatically. The types of auto start entry points available to the attacker depends on level of authorization that the attacker has when installing the implant. Without use of an elevation of privilege exploit, standard users should only be able to create auto start entries which enable the malware to run in their user context. In contrast, users with administrative authorization can create auto start entries which run in the context of the system or any user they choose.

The following list comprises a few of the common auto start entry points utilized in Windows operating systems:

- Scheduled Tasks
- Services
- Drivers
- File associations
- Run and RunOnce registry keys

Delivery Mechanism

Implants can be delivered using a variety of techniques: in the subsections that follow, we will cover a few of the more common ones. The delivery mechanism's purpose is to copy down the implant code, configure any auto start entry points, and hide necessary files. The delivery mechanism is effectively the installer for the malware. Additionally, these delivery mechanisms can be used in succession to further obfuscate the installation process.

Many of these delivery mechanisms are utilized to decrease the likelihood of antivirus detection: it is typically easier to modify the delivery mechanism than to change the implant itself. Once executed, these delivery mechanisms may also disable antimalware or prevent its detection of the implant prior to installation.

Trojan Downloader

A Trojan downloader is a very common delivery mechanism that connects to a server to obtain the implant code. Once launched, a Trojan downloader will connect to a pre-configured network location to download and install the implant on the target's machine.

Trojan Dropper

Trojan droppers are like Trojan downloaders with one key difference: the implant is stored within the dropper rather than being downloaded from a server. The implant payload is typically encrypted or obfuscated to reduce likelihood of detection during installation.

Exploited Data File

Data files used for browser plugins (such as Adobe Flash), default file handlers (such as Java), or productivity applications (such as Adobe Acrobat and the Microsoft Office suite) are another common way to install an implant on a target machine. Productivity applications are ideal targets for phishing campaigns and might be sent to a user as an attachment with an intriguing title.

Attacks against web browsers and browser plugins are typically targeted for installation via a compromised or malicious website. These delivery mechanisms typically load covertly when the website is accessed using a vulnerable browser or browser plugin.

Default file associations target vulnerable applications that are typically associated with a file of a given extension. Operating systems use file extensions to improve user experience – they are what allow you to double click on a ".doc" file and have it magically open in Word, or whatever your default editor is for the ".doc" extension.

Unfortunately, file extension defaults provide an ideal manner to exploit a vulnerable installation of that application. For example, an attacker can send a user target a specially-crafted ".pdf" file and be relatively confident that it will be launched using Adobe Acrobat or Acrobat Reader. Knowing this, the attacker may be able to leverage a vulnerability in that software package to install an implant on the machine.

Software Bundler

A software bundler adds the implant to an existing software package, thus creating a new executable that covertly delivers the implant while masquerading as a perfectly legitimate application. This approach is commonly used with application install packages.

Examples of Notable Implants

To help understand how these pieces all come together we will discuss some implementations of notable implants. The following descriptions are not designed to be full malware write-ups, but are being used to demonstrate the level of sophistication involved in modern targeted attack techniques. To learn more about these implants, one could simply research the provided malware family name.

PlugX

Advanced attackers commonly use their own custom developed implant techniques that sometimes load using non-standard means. One example of a Trojan backdoor which uses a novel loading technique is the PlugX family of implant.

The PlugX family takes advantage of how applications load their dependent libraries when launched. In a PlugX implant, a legitimate library used by the host application is replaced with an implant library of the same name. When the host application loads, the masquerading library is loaded in place of the legitimate library, thus allowing the backdoor to execute in secrecy. An analyst looking for a malicious implant would see nothing other than a legitimate application being loaded and would need to parse the imports table (the table containing the list of libraries that the application will load) and subsequently identify the masquerading library to know it was an implant.

It is important to note that the technique utilized by the PlugX family does not provide any advantage from an access or authorization perspective beyond that of any other form of backdoor. PlugX, like other Trojan malware, is designed to provide durable access to the infected machine using a covert command and control channel. This malware is very difficult to detect since the auto-start mechanism points to a seemingly legitimate application.

Gatak \ Stegoloader

The Gatak Trojan is a malware implant commonly associated with an advanced and highly organized hacking group. This implant is typically installed using a software bundler and various key generators or activation hacking tools.

Once installed, Gatak hides in the user profile and masquerades as one of three applications:

- Skype
- AdVantage
- GoogleTalk

When the user logs on, the application is launched and injects code into another running process for covert execution. Once injected, the originating executable is deleted from disk, thus making it difficult to detect.

The Gatak implant is also notorious for its manner of command and control, leveraging encryption and steganography to covertly hide its communication within PNG formatted images.

Another key differentiator in the Gatak Trojan is its propagation model. Unlike other advanced hacking groups which typically seed very few systems, the group which utilizes the Gatak implant is commonly seeds a very large number of endpoints in an environment of interest.

Powessere \ Poweliks

The Powessere and Poweliks families of implants take a novel approach in how they load. Many blogs discussing these implants refer to them as not being resident on disk; however, this is somewhat of an inaccuracy. A more accurate description is that the malcode in these implants does not have an entry on the file system – they are instead found in registry keys.

The novel portion of the Powessere family of implant is that it can load an executable into memory without referencing a file on the file system. Instead, these implants decode a value stored in registry keys and utilize PowerShell to decode and inject the PE file into memory and begin its execution.

Strengths and Weaknesses

Defending against or evicting a targeted attacker from an enterprise network requires a significant understanding of the strengths and weaknesses of each position. Attackers are typically aware of their strengths and their target's weaknesses, whereas defenders typically are left trying to figure out their battlefield during an incident response – when the damage has already been done. This chapter will discuss the various relevant interests for each party and describe how each party can use them to their advantage.

The Hacker

Hackers have a wide degree of freedom in their arsenal. Unlike defenders, a hacker can (and typically will) resort to abstract forms of attack to which the defenders may be unaware they are vulnerable. This abstract nature provides a lot of freedom in how the attacker operates.

Process and Procedure

Unlike defenders, a hacker is not constrained by policies governing the use of their target's enterprise. This freedom is what enables their agility and allows them to respond to changes in the target's detective capabilities so rapidly.

The hacker is keenly aware that the target's information security team must obtain approvals, change request authorization, and implement other forms of litigation to perform a significant change on the network, such as execution of an eviction plan. Armed with this knowledge, they are typically able to detect upcoming changes and respond accordingly to ensure they maintain their embedded state.

Monitoring Communications

Once an attacker is embedded sufficiently within an enterprise they will be able to monitor communications in various forms. This ability can provide great insight into determining whether they have been detected, monitoring upcoming plans for eviction, and of course performing espionage. For example, an unencrypted email to a company's information security team about an implant discovered by the system's administration team would alert the attackers that they are likely to lose their emplacement and should install a new implant (ideally of a different type) on another server to ensure they do not lose access.

It is important to note that once a system or principal has been sufficiently compromised, the attacker will be able to utilize whatever accesses are afforded to that system or principal. For example,

- If a compromised computer has a microphone attached, the attacker can listen
- If a compromised computer has a camera attached, the attacker can take pictures or record video
- If a compromised user can read an email or a document so can the attacker
- If a compromised computer has any form of input device, the attacker can monitor it

In short, the capability of the attacker is equal to or greater than the assets the attacker possesses. Additionally, because there is no applicable governing policy over the attacker's use of the compromised system, they can typically utilize the system in ways that would be deemed unauthorized for an official user.

On a related side note, many people will utilize a sticker to cover the camera attached to their computer but neglect to disable the microphone. The microphone poses a far more significant risk in that it can record conversations in the room which are likely to provide a much greater value for intelligence gathering than most images. In comparison, the camera can typically only capture what it is aimed at, which is (in many cases) the user.

Abstract Techniques

Attackers work without concern for organizational policy and therefore may be able to utilize techniques which are not authorized for normal use in the environment. Tools used by the attacker may range from normal administration tools, such as the SysInternals suite, all the way to purpose-built weaponized applications, such as Windows Credential Editor.

In some ways, these techniques can give the attackers more "power" than the most senior administrators of the enterprise in that they are more capable because of their tooling. This provides the attackers with a competitive edge over the defender who uses approved tools in the interest of ensuring uptime, adhering to policy, maintaining configuration standardization, and other concerns regarding service health.

Needle in a Haystack

Attackers benefit from the large number of systems within an enterprise boundary. Most attackers purposely choose to infect a select few computers from their target's network to remain covert. This approach makes detection of an implant quite difficult – they could effectively be anywhere. Additionally, this technique makes it difficult to determine if every implant from a targeted attack has been removed: even a single functional implant can allow the attacker reentry into the enterprise and the opportunity to completely change attack signatures.

The Defender

Although attackers have many valuable assets available to them, there are also some very significant advantages available to the defender.

Knowledge of the Network

Although an attacker can learn about a target's network through reconnaissance, the defender typically has a very thorough understanding of their network. Typically, a defender has spent years managing a network and has teams of professionals that know how each service normally operates. In contrast, the attacker must search for documents depicting the design of the network, perform scanning and propagation, and execute other fingerprinting and profiling techniques to learn how the network operates. These behaviors must also remain undetected by intrusion detection systems, antivirus software, and the like.

Legitimate Authorization

Unlike an attacker, the defender has legitimate authorization to their network. This authorization provides a vantage point for the defender if it is not lost to the attacker in the process. Maintaining confidentiality of authenticators as well as integrity of principles authorized for use with these high value credentials is crucial to maintaining this advantage.

Anomaly Detection

Defenders should have a good idea of what their service looks like during normal operation. Details such as traffic patterns, installed applications, performance, credential usage, and the like enable defenders to create a baseline from which they can identify anomalies.

When an attacker infects a machine with an implant, it must have some form of auto-start capability and must have some means to communicate to a command and control server for it to be of use. A perceptive defender can identify these differences and identify the attacker's presence once detected.

Stealth

Stealth is an asset available to both attackers and defenders if leveraged properly. An attacker leverages stealth by hiding among the many systems throughout the enterprise, by being cautious not to cause significant operational impact, through validating that their tools are not detected before use, and by operating outside of normal working hours. An attacker skilled with stealth will be much less likely to be caught than one that sets off alerts throughout the organization. Once detected, an attacker must change tactics, implants, command and control, etc. to regain stealth and is now more susceptible to subsequent detection due to a heightened level of alert by the defender.

Defenders also must be skilled in stealth to succeed in evicting an embedded attacker from their network. Attackers with sufficient control over an enterprise will be able to monitor activity of the defender to identify if they have been detected. As such, it is ideal to perform all breach notifications, research about an embedded attacker, and eviction planning on an out-of-band network with no security association with the production network. In addition, machines used for this planning should also not be associated with the production network and should be monitored.

Summary

Attackers and defenders each have assets which are available to them if they can leverage them. Being able to leverage these benefits is crucial to the success of that party, especially in the case of the defender. In the coming chapters, we will discuss how to design an enterprise service which enables the defender to maximize their benefits and reduce the utility of the attacker's benefit wherever possible.

So you got Pwned

It happens all too often – suddenly a person in operations opens a ticket to troubleshoot a software issue and discovers malware, or a large amount of funds are unexplainably transferred from the corporate coffers, or perhaps a large amount of data becomes encrypted or goes missing. Sadly, cyberattacks are becoming more common, and it is important to understand how to respond to them.

Dealing with a targeted attack is very different than handling commodity malware (the malicious software one simply stumbles upon on the web occasionally). As previously discussed, addressing a targeted attack situation means addressing the human element as well as the malicious software. A determined human adversary can identify and respond to anomalies such as a handful of systems suddenly going offline, or one of their credentials becoming suddenly invalidated.

Successful eviction of a targeted attacker requires comprehensive planning and rapid execution. This section will discuss the intricacies involved in detecting attacker implants and ultimately evicting the emplaced attacker.

Performing an Incident Response

The first step in responding to any targeted attack is performing an incident response assessment. An incident response answers crucial questions about an attack. At a minimum, an incident response for a targeted attack should provide the ABC's of the event:

- **A**ccounts utilized by or exposed to the attacker
- **B**ackdoors identified on the network
- **C**ommand and control channels used by backdoors

Additionally, an incident response commonly provides information about how the attacker entered the network, what may have been stolen or tampered with, and what actor group association may exist when sufficient intelligence exists to make a determination.

Incident response is a field which has changed significantly over its existence. Early incident response focused on performing a thorough analysis of disk images to extract very comprehensive timelines containing lots of evidence surrounding activity performed by the attacker during the compromise. This approach is still leveraged in prosecution and other legal proceedings due to its thoroughness and focus on chain of custody and forensic integrity.

Through time, targeted attackers became more agile and spread throughout the network more rapidly. This change caused a problem with traditional forensics: by the time the forensic analyst discovered what other machines, accounts, or implants may be involved, the attacker was already many steps ahead. As such, the incident response process had to adapt to become much faster.

Current (as of the writing of this book) incident response teams typically take a breadth before depth approach to analysis: they cover as many machines as possible searching for indicators of compromise, rather than finding one machine at a time and performing a thorough dead box analysis of it. The breadth first approach enables rapid correlation of indicators of compromise (network communications, file attributes, account usage, etc.), thus enabling the incident response team to actively hunt attackers on a network. Traditional forensics is still quite valuable in insider threat, legal proceedings, and other situations where detailed information about activity is more valued than agility of detection.

Bring in the Experts

Targeted attacker implants are typically very hard to find without specialized tooling and unique skillsets. As such, it is important to engage a specialist incident response team early to determine the extent of compromise.

Incident response companies are generally on the forefront of the targeted attack world – they have access to the latest indicators of compromise and techniques used by advanced attackers. Additionally, these teams have special purpose-built toolsets and capabilities as well as access to private data sources which enable them to rapidly classify findings.

Third, malware used in a targeted attack is typically very difficult to disassemble – with a heavy focus on protecting the command and control information. Professional incident response teams typically employ reverse engineers with a specialization in taking apart highly obfuscated or encrypted malware.

If possible, it may be wise to bring in more than one incident response team with different specializations. For example, one incident response team may specialize in host-based analysis, such as identifying anomalous programs running on machines, whereas another may be more skilled in network traffic analysis, including finding command and control infrastructure from network traffic captures. When paired, these two teams can complement each other and can provide indicators of compromise to enhance the detective capability of the other team.

The Art of Remediation

Once the incident response event is complete, it is time to begin developing a plan of how to evict the emplaced attacker. One of the best cybersecurity books that you can refer to when performing an eviction was written in the 5th century BC – Sun Tzu's famous The Art of War.

It is worth reiterating that you are not simply removing software, but rather a human who has established control over your environment. As such, you are effectively evicting an army who has successfully infiltrated your base and may have similar authorization as your most senior administrators. For this reason, The Art of War provides great insight into how to deal with the human aspect of the reclamation event.

Tipping Your Hand

"Let your plans be dark and impenetrable as night, and when you move, fall like a thunderbolt." – Sun Tzu

One of the most important tenets of a successful eviction is avoiding what is referred to "tipping your hand": showing your intentions to the attacker prior to execution. Stealth is one of the most important attributes of both parties – the target and the attacker. An attacker must remain hidden to avoid detection, while a defender's intentions and detections must remain concealed from the attacker. Unfortunately, the latter is more difficult when the attacker has administrative access to the target's network.

Maintaining stealth means establishing a separate infrastructure for communications surrounding the incident response and eviction efforts. Depending on which credentials are breached, an attacker may be able to monitor e-mail or IM communications, log keystrokes, or read data from secure locations on the network. This means that ensuring stealth will require a separate communication infrastructure that does not share authorization with the existing compromised network. Additionally, it is ideal to utilize machines that do not trust authorization from the compromised network (i.e., not domain members of a compromised domain).

Bias for Action

"When campaigning, be swift as the wind." – Sun Tzu

Another important attribute of a successful eviction effort is speed. If remediation efforts are implemented slowly, an attacker is likely to detect them and change techniques to maintain persistence. To avoid this, the organization performing the eviction must perform sufficient planning ahead of time to ensure speed when executing the recovery effort.

Seek a Comprehensive and Well-Planned Eviction Strategy

"The supreme art of war is to subdue the enemy without fighting." – Sun Tzu

Ultimately, the goal is to catch the attacker off-guard and perform an eviction with as little risk of response or retaliation as possible. Accomplishing this means focusing on maintaining stealth and maximizing speed. Additionally, it is important to ensure that you truly understand the method that the attacker is using to maintain access and authorization to your enterprise.

Think Like a Hacker

"To know your Enemy, you must become your Enemy." – Sun Tzu

It is difficult to defend against or evict an attacker when you do not fully understand their capabilities. As the title of this book suggests, you must think like a hacker to defend against or successfully evict a hacker. It is necessary to ensure that the staff performing an eviction truly understands what capabilities the attacker has; otherwise, the defenses and activities being implemented may fall short of successfully evicting the attacker from the network.

Thinking like a hacker means studying the tooling that hackers use, attending hacker conferences such as DEFCON, and practicing hacking and exploitation in a lab environment. A thorough understanding of a hacker's capabilities and techniques will help your organization establish an effective defensive posture, detect relevant threats earlier, and improve the likelihood of a successful eviction.

Be Prepared for Retaliation

"Victorious warriors win first and then go to war, while defeated warriors go to war first and then seek to win" – Sun Tzu

More than likely, the attackers do not want to lose their foothold in your environment. If cleanup is not performed as a planned and concerted effort, it is likely that the attackers will respond to their detection in one of multiple ways:

- They may change the machines where their implants are installed
- They may become destructive to prevent forensics or in vengeance
- They may change their implant technique to one which differs from those currently in use, thus potentially reestablishing their stealth

Evicting the Attacker

The first step to a successful reclamation event is not action: blocking a command and control channel, removing an implant, or resetting stolen administrator credentials is likely to breach the defender's stealth and cause the attacker to change their techniques, thus requiring further investigation. Instead of acting, it is important to utilize the indicators of compromise (IOC's) from the incident response work to establish passive monitoring. This monitoring should enable any defender to do the following:

- See when a command and control channel is used
- Discover installation of new backdoors
- Identify when a known malicious application or technique is utilized
- Establish monitoring of known stolen accounts to determine if they become compromised after the reclamation takes place

Monitoring the attacker's activity prior to reclamation is of limited utility outside of monitoring for interaction with high value servers – more than likely, they have access to much of the network already and have authorization to perform a wide range of activities on the enterprise. Additionally, aside from knowing what data was breached, there are very few activities that an attacker can perform that would fundamentally change the recovery plan.

Efforts to evict the attacker should focus on eliminating the two aspects that an attacker needs to maintain control over an asset: access and authorization. All reclamation activities should be implemented in coordinated and rapid succession to limit the attacker's ability to respond to the effort by re-infecting hosts or by changing implant techniques or command and control infrastructure.

Establishing an Order of Operations

A reclamation event should follow a very strict order of operations, beginning with the most valuable systems and credentials and working towards the least valuable. In all cases, any administrative credentials to authentication or authorization infrastructure should be considered most valuable – all other efforts will fail without confidence in authentication or authorization.

Second, the organization should focus on any systems which hold information deemed critical to business operations. Systems in this list house information which, if stolen, leaked, or tampered with, would significantly hinder organizational operations or competitive ability. It is typically best to obtain a list of these systems from the perspective of executive management rather than from IT operations as IT management's prioritization typically aligns with a different set of needs.

Finally, any other systems and credentials within scope of the breach should be addressed. Never underestimate the power of a standard domain user account: in many organizations a regular user with their group membership has access and authorization to very sensitive information and abilities. Although last in succession, it is important to address these assets comprehensively as reclamation cannot be guaranteed unless all potentially stolen credentials are reset and all known compromised machines addressed.

Elimination of Backdoors

Backdoors installed by an attacker can be complex and difficult to remove. Tools, such as rootkits, can be leveraged to hide implant locations and prevent removal. As such, the generic recommendation for any targeted attacker implants is a complete rebuild of the affected machine.

In situations where a rebuild is not feasible, it is recommended to utilize an antivirus product to clean the implant. Antimalware products are designed to deal with removal of malicious software; thus, they are more likely to successfully remove a backdoor than simply deleting known files.

In many cases, the antimalware product may not identify the backdoor as being malicious without explicit submission of the implant to the antimalware company. This submission should be performed in concert with other reclamation activities to maintain stealth. Early submission of the implant to an antivirus company can alert the attackers to the target's knowledge of their persistence, causing them to change implant techniques and possibly command and control infrastructure to reestablish stealth.

If data from the compromised system will be migrated to a new machine as part of the rebuild process, all migrated files should be scanned using antivirus software with signatures that include all known attacker implants.

Execution

When ready, reclamation should begin by blocking all known access to command and control channels. Blocking access should be performed both locally and within the enterprise, since a laptop removed from the environment could reconnect to attacker command and control infrastructure. Blocking access to command and control channels ensures that the attacker is unable to control implants, forcing them to rely on stolen credentials for authorization and only publicly available access points. Depending on the credentials stolen by the attacker and externally-available interfaces, the attacker may be forced completely out of the environment once command and control is severed.

Second, it is necessary to begin reclaiming all credentials and systems in the domain using the previously-identified order of operations. Following the order of operations will ensure that the most valuable credentials to an attacker are eliminated first, thus rapidly limiting the value of any stolen credentials in value order.

At this point, the attackers should no longer have control over any implants (eliminating the associated access and authorization) or accounts (eliminating the associated authorization). Any new implants they attempt to install which utilize the known command and control infrastructure can be identified by attempts to connect to the command and control point and will fail to connect (if implemented properly).

What's Next?

At this point, if the attackers have vested interest in staying embedded on the network, they are likely to quickly begin a campaign to attempt to regain access and authorization within the network. As such, it is important to monitor the enterprise for potential breach and ensure users are trained to avoid falling for phishing tactics which could lead to breach.

Ultimately, the best solution for reducing the impact of a targeted attack lies in the information system architecture. Effective enterprise design assumes breach and limits the impact of compromise by reducing the value of a standard workstation and focusing security investment on the server infrastructure. In the coming chapters we will discuss how to design an enterprise network to be as resilient as possible to targeted attack.

Designing an Access and Authorization Strategy

Earlier in the book we discussed how all hacking can be distilled into two core concepts – access and authorization. The following sections will take a deeper dive into how these concepts can be implemented in the most effective way possible.

A proper access control strategy should enable unencumbered use to legitimate users of the service while highlighting any attempts to breach or misuse the service whenever possible. Additionally, these protections should not cause significant overhead to systems administrators or information security professionals monitoring the enterprise.

A Brief History of Access Control

During the evolution of IT, access control was commonly the go-to method for controlling the security of a service. In early iterations of enterprise networks, remote access was impossible or very difficult. Computers were large, the Internet was not readily available, and ultimately the walls of the building itself that housed the computers provided sufficient protection as there were few services that could be accessed remotely. Early forms of remote access were provided by banks of modems in datacenters which required any users who accessed them to know the phone number for the modem bank as well as a set of valid credentials.

As the Internet came about and businesses began to see the value of publishing services externally (such as websites, email, and the like), the need to be increasingly more connected caused a shift in how network protection was considered. Forward-thinking businesses during this timeframe created the concept of a demilitarized zone, or DMZ. In a DMZ, Internet-facing servers are separated from the internal network as well as the Internet using firewalls – purpose built devices designed to govern access to servers, typically based on rules outlining permitted or blocked pairs of source and destination network addresses and ports. During this time, laptops became more common and remote access evolved to using encryption to virtually connect a computer to the corporate network using a virtual private network, or VPN.

Sometime around this period in history, the Internet became available to more and more employees within their corporate network. Firewalls were heavily focused on limiting inbound traffic – traffic sourcing from the Internet and connecting to servers housed in the DMZ; however, little thought was provided to vulnerabilities sourced from internal users connecting outbound to the Internet. This condition brought about malware infections, social engineering, and other attacks against internal users. Thus, industry began developing antimalware software to protect from viruses, proxy servers to govern internet browsing, and website reputation services to assist organizations in attempting to classify website content automatically. Unfortunately, the task of maintaining a list of websites proved quite unwieldy.

Further evolutions increased the number of applications that benefitted from remote connectivity, the numbers of personal computers increased significantly, and non-PC devices, namely Blackberry phones, began to benefit from connectivity to corporate resources. This transformation also meant that organizational data was now being stored on portable devices, which posed an entirely new category of risk. Additionally, business partnerships and customer portals caused more and more holes to be punched in the connection between the DMZ and the internal network, thus causing the monolithic style of network architecture to become less effective.

Today, we live in a world where personal devices are regularly connected to corporate resources. People expect to be able to work from nearly everywhere using nearly every device, regardless of corporate ownership. Instant messages are used for corporate communication and provide for virtual meeting spaces, virtual telephone numbers, and other services to both employees and partners. Organizations struggle with maintaining access control changes involved in mergers, acquisitions, and partnerships where one organization's information systems are assimilated into another's enterprise.

Additionally, hackers are keenly aware of the monolithic design of most enterprises – a design which places nearly every user's workstation within the boundary of the organization's firewalls. Those firewalls must be able to support all ingress and egress traffic sourcing from tens to hundreds of thousands of users being productive and using corporate services as well as public-facing services to continue business. Additionally, attempting to pick out malicious network communications from the gigabytes of network traffic occurring between systems within the enterprise is like trying to find a needle in a haystack.

Controlling access as a form of security is a nightmare due to today's highly-connected nature – or is it?

A Pragmatic Approach to Service Security

Limiting access to a service has a very direct cost associated with it: legitimate access to services becomes quite difficult and many times requires the use of confusing network technology. Additionally, such limited access often causes administrative overhead, trouble calls from users, computers with bifurcated configurations to support both connected and disconnected states, and expectations that every user must understand network technology to some level to be productive.

The cost associated with a network architecture that focuses on providing security through access limitation can be expressed in trouble tickets, lost productivity, capital expenses from larger network security components, competitive advantage, difficulty hiring, reduced tenure, reduced strategic agility, and many other sources. To be competitive in today's world, we must be connected.

Implementing security through limiting accessibility should occur only in the following situations:

- When the service being secured provides little or no benefit to standard users of the system
- When the confidentiality of the service being protected outweighs the benefit of its accessibility to users
- When access limitations are implemented on interfaces not employed by a normal user (i.e. administrative interfaces)

In contrast, protecting a service through authorization control provides a much more sustainable solution. Controlling authorization places significant weight on ensuring the integrity of the authentication service – a concern that exists regardless of extraneous security measures taken to protect administrative interfaces. Additionally, software vulnerability and proper systems development lifecycle come to the forefront, as a vulnerability in public-facing interfaces can provide hackers access and authorization through software exploitation.

Controlling Security through Authorization

Implementing security through authorization control means placing significant trust in the service providing authorization. As such, it is critical that authentication and authorization systems be held to a high standard of change management to ensure unintended security holes do not manifest. Additionally, it is important not to forget the concepts behind vulnerability chaining when performing this analysis: the ability to control a principal with authorization to an identified account is equivalent to acting as the principal itself. This section will discuss some of the various rules that should be followed to avoid vulnerability in authorization control.

Rule 1: Monitor Direct Administrative Authorization to the Service

Authentication and authorization services have many necessary forms of authorization which, if abused, can be leveraged to compromise the integrity of the service itself. Many of these forms of authorization are provided to well-known principals within the service; however, in many cases this authorization can be delegated explicitly, thus obscuring the total breadth of principals with significant authorization within the service.

Examples of administrative authorization to an authentication or authorization service may include any of the following:

- Authorization to replicate account secrets, which can be used to steal credentials to accounts authenticated by the authentication service
- Authorization to trust outside authentication services, which can be used to establish illegitimate authentication to the service, and possibly to services which trust the service for authentication
- Authorization to replicate changes to the service itself, which can be used to covertly create, delete, or modify principals in the authentication or authorization service
- Authorization to add a replica server in an authentication or authorization service, which can be used to replicate sensitive data to an attacker-controlled system
- Authorization to change access control lists which provide any form of administrative authorization to the service, which can be leveraged to grant new authorization

Rule 2: Monitor Administrative Authorization to Servers Providing the Service

Any server which hosts the authentication or authorization service has the potential of compromising the confidentiality or integrity of the service itself. These principals can bypass protections provided by the service through manipulating the environment in which it operates. As with services, many of these forms of authorization are provided to explicit groups, but can be (and commonly are) modified to provide explicit authorization to other principals.

Some examples of administrative authorization to an operating system include the following:

- Authorization to back up files, which can be used to read account credentials or other sensitive information regardless of access control lists on the files themselves
- Authorization to restore files, which can be used to overwrite sensitive service files regardless of access control lists on the files themselves
- Authorization to read or write system memory (i.e. perform operating system debugging), which can be used to read and write sensitive portions of service memory
- Authorization to load software or drivers which have access to operating system memory, which provides an equivalent level of authorization as debugging
- Authorization to impersonate users on an operating system, which can be used to act on behalf of any account which is logged on to the machine
- Authorization to take ownership of objects, which can be used to bypass access control to objects controlled by the operating system

Rule 3: Monitor Recursive Membership of Administrative Groups

Grouping improves manageability of authorization control; however, grouping can also be used to obscure the true number of administrative principals which exist in an enterprise. Additionally, any principals nested within groups who are delegated administrative authorization must be protected at the same level as all other administrative principals for the authentication or authorization service.

Rule 4: Monitor Cross-Service Administrative Principals

In some cases, cross-service trusts provide accounts from a different authentication or authorization service than would administrative authorization to the service itself. In those situations, any compromise of the trusted service can translate into compromise of the service itself. For example, any of the following scenarios may occur:

- If a compromised user account in a trusted authentication service has administrative authorization to the trusting authentication or authorization service, the attacker can use that authorization
- If a user account is maintained by a trusted, but compromised, authentication service, the attacker can masquerade as the trusted user to obtain authorization to the service
- If a group maintained by a trusted, but compromised, authorization service is delegated administrative authorization to the service, the

attacker can manipulate membership of that group to provide administrative authorization to the service
- If any of the previously mentioned situations provide authorization to a server providing the service rather than to the service itself, the attacker can utilize that authorization to compromise the server

As such, if cross-domain delegation of administrative authorization is necessary, administrative authorization to the trusted authentication or authorization service must be protected at the same level or higher than the service.

The Monolithic Model

In a monolithic model, all credentials and authorization are controlled in one place. In Active Directory or Kerberos terms, this would be equivalent to a single domain architecture. Most organizations leverage a monolithic model in their design because this model is simple and easy to understand. Additionally, this model fits well with the traditional "build a wall around it" approach to security: we know where the sensitive information is and we can therefore implement defense in depth.

Monolithic Architecture
- All users authenticated and authorized by the same system
- Servers and workstations authentication and authorization performed by same system
- Multiple sources may be used, but authentication and authorization is intermingled
---

Figure 5 Monolithic Architecture

Basic credential hygiene can be implemented in a monolithic architecture through controlling which accounts can log on to which machines. For example, we can identify a subset of machines as being used to administer the domain and prevent those accounts from logging on to non-administrative machines. We can also prevent accounts which are not administrative in nature from logging on to machines used to perform administration, thus limiting the likelihood that a normal user account, if compromised, could perform malicious activity on a machine used for administration. This design can be utilized somewhat effectively and is especially helpful when a very complex authorization structure is already in place.

Unfortunately, the monolithic model poses significant risk to an organization in the event of compromise. First, if any administrative credentials are stolen, the entire authentication \ authorization infrastructure becomes at-risk and can no longer be trusted. Fighting an adversary having the same amount of power in your organization as your most senior administrators is quite difficult and not recommended.

Second, credential hygiene is only a façade in a hic architecture – one that is easy to bypass given enough legitimate authorization. Additionally, it is difficult to be confident that you truly know all your administrative accounts in a monolithic architecture. Over time, regular accounts can gain significant power within the domain through delegation, resulting in administrative accounts of which administrators are not aware.

Multiple monolithic domains (such as having a "DMZ" domain) can provide some protection against attackers targeting those public-facing resources; however, in these designs it is common to find cross-domain trusts which delegate authority between the authorization domains which can then be used to provide authorization to the trusting domain.

Controlling authorization within a monolithic model is almost not possible because all services share the same authentication and authorization service. Compromise of a single user or computer can lead to compromise of the entire network, thus making every machine and user very important. Ultimately, this means investing a large amount of time, effort, and resources to protect the entire network equally.

The Tiered Authentication Model

One way to address the concerns associated with a monolithic architecture is to utilize a tiered authentication model, like the model proposed by a mandatory access control (MAC) system. In a tiered system, highly valued credentials are entrusted to an external authentication service (i.e., separate domain). Policy is configured to prevent credential exposure outside of necessity, and thus administrative credentials maintain their confidentiality.

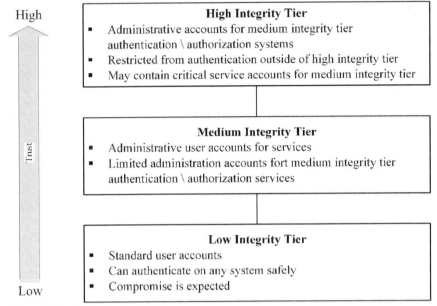

Figure 6. Tiered Authentication Model

For a tiered authentication model to be successful, all credentials to the system providing administrative authorization to the service must be restricted from exposure to lower tiered systems. This is not to be confused with the multiple monolithic domain architecture; this design focuses on the value of the credential as its basis for where it is exposed rather than the risk of exposure of the systems that are a part of the domain.

The tiered authentication design is very effective at limiting credential exposure at the cost of some administrative overhead. Additionally, and most importantly, this design assumes that the lowest integrity tier will be breached and designs protections commensurate with the risk level associated with that tier. When this occurs, the attackers should not be able to steal credentials which provide them administrative authorization to the tier, therefore limiting their authorization and making remediation simpler.

Although the tiered model is effective at protecting credentials, there are a few drawbacks in its implementation. To begin with, a tiered model suffers a similar issue as a monolithic architecture in that all administrative credentials exist in the same tier. A compromise of a higher tier (for example, a password being saved in a file readable by a lower tier) can result in a compromise of all credentials protected at that tier.

Secondly, the tiered model may require a lot of users to have many accounts to maintain. Depending on implementation, a user may have a different account within each tier to manage the tier below it. The large number of credentials associated with this design increases administrative overhead and can result in increased licensing, hardware costs, and delays.

Finally, controlling administrative access to services in a tiered model is difficult. Much like the monolithic model, there are many holes that must be punched through the firewall for different services to operate. This translates to difficulty in manageability, a reduced access posture, and a larger number of in-roads that an attacker can use to take over a tier.

Service-Centric Architecture

Service-centric architecture differs from a tiered model in that there is not a single hierarchy of trust. Instead, user authorization is outsourced to one or more trusted authentication providers, whereas administrative authorization is contained within the service itself and not outsourced to other providers.

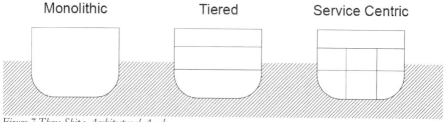

Figure 7 Three Ships Architectural Analogy

One way to visualize these architectural concepts would be to think of three ships with different bulkhead (wall) configurations.

Using this analogy, a monolithic architecture would be equivalent to having a hull with no bulkheads within it to separate compartments (equivalent to utilizing a single authentication and authorization service for your entire enterprise). In this condition, any breach of the hull would result in water flooding the interior of the ship, ultimately resulting in the ship sinking.

A ship mirroring the tiered model would utilize multiple decks (floors) within the hull, but still no bulkheads. In this model, the impact of a breach within a lower tier system affects all authentication and authorization within that tier, but is prevented from moving upwards – assuming the model was implemented properly.

Our third ship is the service centric ship. In this design, multiple bulkheads are implemented, thus further localizing the impact of a hull breach to only the affected compartment. Placement of the bulkheads in this ship represent the administrative boundaries of services. This reflects an ideal concept for security design as long as we are mindful to limit administrative overhead (the number of bulkheads that an employee in one compartment would need to traverse on a regular basis). If too many bulkheads are implemented, administrators are likely to leave "doors" open between compartments to reduce administrative overhead.

What is a service?

The first step in service-centric architecture is identifying a service. A service is a group of highly-integrated software packages which provide a cohesive capability. Services commonly share a team of administrators: an administrator in one software package within a service likely has elevated authorization to other software packages within the same service.

Some examples of services may include the following:

- User authentication
- A website or web farm
- Email
- An enterprise resource planning (ERP) system
- A line of business software system
- A security event and incident management system
- Voice over IP (VoIP)

Example: E-mail Service

In an e-mail service, the core capability supported by the system would be communication and collaboration. In addition to e-mail servers, you are likely to find other services such as the following:

- Spam filtering
- E-mail archiving
- E-discovery
- Instant messaging
- Conference services

The description of what an e-mail service looks like will differ between organizations depending on what services are integrated with the e-mail \ communications system – in some organizations, conferencing software and instant messaging may warrant their own distinct services depending on integration and administrative overlap.

Boundaries of an e-mail service are defined by disparate administrators and integration over communication channels that are normally public. For example, if a website needs to send e-mail to its users, it is likely to use the SMTP protocol. An e-mail service must provide a public SMTP interface to enable it to receive e-mail; therefore, the integration between the website and the e-mail service is entirely over public ports and protocols. It is also unlikely that e-mail will share the same administrators in an organization of any size; therefore, administration should be segmented. We can confidently say that the website and e-mail are two disparate services since all integration occurs over publicly accessible ports and protocols, and administration is not shared between the website and the e-mail service.

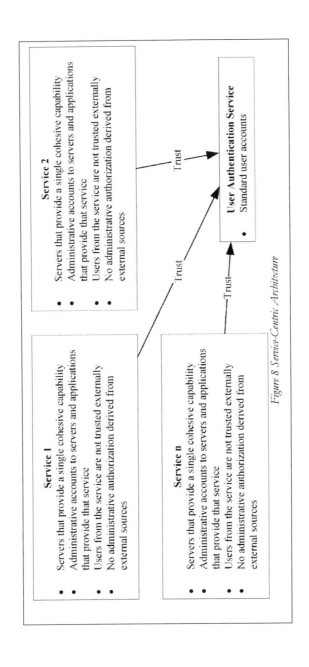

Figure 8 Service-Centric Architecture

Service 1

- Servers that provide a single cohesive capability
- Administrative accounts to servers and applications that provide that service
- Users from the service are not trusted externally
- No administrative authorization derived from external sources

Service 2

- Servers that provide a single cohesive capability
- Administrative accounts to servers and applications that provide that service
- Users from the service are not trusted externally
- No administrative authorization derived from external sources

Service n

- Servers that provide a single cohesive capability
- Administrative accounts to servers and applications that provide that service
- Users from the service are not trusted externally
- No administrative authorization derived from external sources

User Authentication Service

- Standard user accounts

Trust

Trust

Trust

Applying Service-Centric Architecture

In service-centric architecture, authentication and authorization are provided by two distinct sources: credentials that translate into user-level authorization within the service, and those that translate to administrative authorization. Credentials that translate to user authorization within the system are provided by an external authentication source. Any credentials that translate to administrative authorization within the service are maintained by a separate authentication and authorization system that is contained within the service.

The split authentication model simplifies tracking of accounts, while also limiting the impact of stolen credentials. If the user authentication service is compromised, the most authority an attacker can obtain is that of any standard user maintained by that service. For an attacker to obtain a credential with administrative authorization to the service, they must compromise a system within the service – a much more challenging task. Administrative accounts for the service are not trusted by other domains, thus limiting their exposure significantly.

In the event of service compromise, service-centric architecture also limits the scope of the compromise to a single service, rather than to an entire tier or the entire monolithic authorization domain. Using this model, we can reduce the breadth of scope of administrative accounts to within a given service. These accounts will also benefit from limited exposure since they are not trusted outside the service.

Overhead in this model is also reduced, since the service has a dedicated source for administrative authentication and authorization. In a monolithic or tiered model, delegations must be carefully monitored to ensure that they do not bleed over between services and accidentally provide unintended authorization. In a service-centric architecture, the most authorization that one could be delegated is still limited within their service, thus limiting impact and eliminating widespread administrative accounts.

High security environments can utilize a hybrid model whereby access to accounts with administrative authority to the service's authentication and authorization system are provided by a higher tier authentication source. In this instance, a compromise of a service will not lead to a compromise of the authentication and authorization service itself – thus preventing password dumping or other vulnerabilities that manifest when an authentication system is compromised.

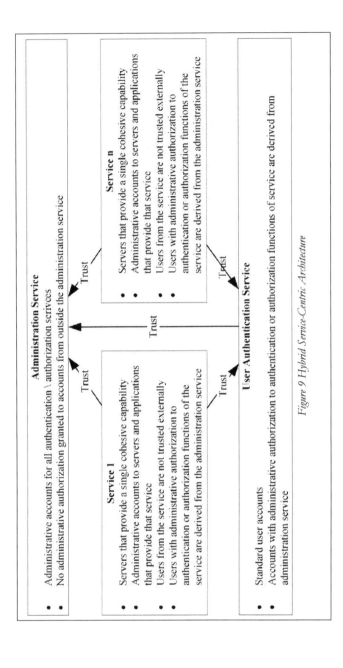

Administration Service

- Administrative accounts for all authentication \ authorization serivces
- No administrative authorization granted to accounts from outside the administration service

Service 1

- Servers that provide a single cohesive capability
- Administrative accounts to servers and applications that provide that service
- Users from the service are not trusted externally
- Users with administrative authorization to authentication or authorization functions of the service are derived from the administration service

Service n

- Servers that provide a single cohesive capability
- Administrative accounts to servers and applications that provide that service
- Users from the service are not trusted externally
- Users with administrative authorization to authentication or authorization functions of the service are derived from the administration service

User Authentication Service

- Standard user accounts
- Accounts with administrative authorization to authentication or authorization functions of service are derived from administration service

Trust

Figure 9 Hybrid Service-Centric Architecture

64

Implementing Service-Centric Architecture

Service-centric architecture requires the organization to invest in planning the layout of their information systems prior to implementation. Although it is possible to migrate a service from a monolithic or tiered architecture to a service-centric architecture, it is likely that nearly all of the servers supporting that service will be rebuilt during the process.

The following sections cover the steps required to implement a service-centric architecture in your organization.

Step 1: Define the Service

Defining a service begins by enumerating a list of services provided by the enterprise. Services can include out-of-the-box capabilities (such as email, content management, or IT service management), custom-developed in-house solutions (such as a website provided to allow customers to order products, line-of-business management solutions, or HR solutions), or a hybrid of multiple integrated services designed to provide a single cohesive capability.

A typical service boundary can also be seen organizationally. A properly-defined service will have several highly similar or highly integrated components managed by the same IT staff. Look for teams that share an identity with the service they manage – when you find them, you are likely to have found a service.

Avoid getting too granular during service definition: a service should be broad enough to include all highly-integrated capabilities offered by the enterprise. For example, an authentication service may include certification authorities, credential vault solutions, multi-factor authentication solutions, and\or identity management capabilities.

Step 2: Identify Dependencies

Dependencies are programs which are integrated with the service, but may not be part of the service itself. These services may require special communications between services over non-standard ports or protocols. Where possible, these dependencies should be limited to ensure consistency.

When a dependency is identified, it may be prudent to determine whether the dependent service would be best managed by the team responsible for managing the dependent service, rather than by the team managing the service it was initially identified within.

For example, let's say your team identifies a proxy server and groups it within a service that provides client services (such as patching, updates, support, etc.). In researching dependencies, it is identified that the proxy servers require proprietary integration with servers providing user authentication – an entirely different service. In this instance, it may be easier to move the proxy servers to the user authentication service than to maintain inter-service dependency.

Step 3: Define Necessary Communication for Users

Once a service and its dependencies have been identified, begin looking at communications required for the service to be accessible by standard users of the service. This list should include every form of communication that the service must provide to enable standard users to interface with it; however, the list should not include ports solely used for administration of the service itself or any of its components.

Any communication channels on the list of necessary communication ports should be explicitly whitelisted for outside use to maximize utility wherever possible.

Communication used for administration of the service or its components should be published in some manner that only allows trusted and authenticated entities (administrators) access. This solution may be some form of authenticated reverse proxy, virtual private network (VPN), or the like.

Step 4: Design the Credential Protection Strategy

Now that we have identified how we will secure access to our service, it is time to design our authorization control. Where possible, all credentials and access controls that provide administrative authorization to the service should be authenticated by a dedicated authentication and authorization system within the service. Dedicating a separate authentication and authorization infrastructure prevents credentials with broad administrative authority in other services inheriting administrative authority to a service which should not be in their control.

Users of the service should be authenticated using an authentication service trusted by, but separate from, the service's authentication and authorization system. For example, authentication of administrative users within the domain may be provided by an Active Directory domain, whereas authentication of standard users may occur over a one-way Kerberos trust, federated authentication, or through use of the oAuth protocol with a trusted authentication source.

All administrative accounts for the service should be derived from the authentication and authorization infrastructure housed within the service. Other authentication and authorization services should not trust identities maintained by the service's credential provider – doing so may expose administrative credentials to the service to systems outside of the service, thus enabling credential theft.

Service-Centric Architecture and Active Directory

As of this book, Microsoft's Active Directory is the most popular directory services infrastructure in use. As such, we will discuss some specific nuances related to implementation of service-centric architecture.

The main design component of an Active Directory implementation consists of forests and domains. A forest is the ultimate authentication and authorization boundary of the implementation. External sources can be trusted to provide authentication and group information from externally-trusted sources can be referenced across the trust, if configured properly.

Within the forest, the implementation will consist of one or more domains. A domain is inherently trusted by all other domains in the forest and (by default) serves as an authorization boundary. Additionally, a domain serves as a replication boundary for credentials for principals authenticated by the domain: if an attacker can attain administrative credentials to the domain, they can exfiltrate credentials, thus making the domain untrustworthy for authentication.

User accounts within a domain are automatically part of a special group called "Domain Users" which provides a user the authorization to perform interactive logons to workstations and add computers to the domain. In addition, the group is listed in the built-in "Users" group of every domain member machine.

Another form of default authorization provided within the context of a domain is the "Domain Admins" group. Members of this group are granted membership in the built-in "Administrators" group on every computer in the domain. An administrator possesses a significant amount of authorization to the machine; thus, this group should have few members and its membership should be monitored.

The third (and most powerful) principal to be aware of is the "Enterprise Admins" group. Members of the "Enterprise Admins" group are (by default) granted membership to the "Domain Admins" group in every domain within the forest. This group is only present in the first domain within a forest and should be guarded closely. Additionally, many security-minded organizations will remove the "Enterprise Admins" group from the "Domain Admins" group of every domain within the forest, thus severing authority at the domain boundary.

Another important aspect of an Active Directory forest is its shared configuration partition. The configuration partition contains services which are trusted by all domains within the forest, including information about certificate authorities trusted to provide user authentication certificates, trusted root certification authorities, and forest-wide trust configurations.

Implementing service-centric architecture in an Active Directory model means segmenting each service into separate forests or domains to eliminate authorization inherited by groups granting broad administrative authority, such as the "Domain Admins" group. Utilizing separate forests increases administrative overhead required to manage the Active Directory. Use of separate forests enables the use of one-way trusts which can be used to ensure credentials from one service domain aren't used to grant authorization in other domains and ensure interactive logon with these credentials is not possible.

If a single forest design is used, it is necessary to ensure that the domain containing the "Enterprise Admins" group is used as the most authoritative domain for the enterprise. Services should be implemented as separate domains within the forest and, if possible, all members of the "Domain Admins" group should be sourced from that initial domain, thus creating an "authentication management" service. Additionally, non-domain controller machines should be configured to explicitly prevent interactive logon from any member of the "Domain Admins" group in order to prevent credential theft.

Another important design consideration is the level of exposure to which the Active Directory infrastructure will be subjected. Active Directory requires a very large amount of firewall exceptions to enable replication between domain controllers, authentication, and the like. If the service that utilizes Active Directory is highly exposed, such as web servers hosted in a DMZ, it may be prudent to utilize separate Active Directory forests to reduce the risk to production authentication services.

Designing an Authentication Strategy

Implementing authentication in an enterprise isn't terribly difficult, but implementing an effective, efficient, and secure authentication strategy can be quite difficult without proper understanding of how everything works internally. In this section, we will discuss the components that make up authentication and how to implement them in a manner that provides optimal security and manageability.

An authentication service maintains a mapping between credentials and identities, and may also have a means to convey those identities to other authentication or authorization services cryptographically. Credentials are the means of identifying the principal user to the system, and thus must be sufficiently strong to ensure the authenticity of the principal being identified.

Credentials can be separated into two general categories: symmetric and asymmetric. Both symmetric and asymmetric credentials have their own benefits and drawbacks based on their implementation and the circumstances surrounding their usage.

Symmetric Credentials

A symmetric credential is one where a provided value is compared to an identical or cryptographically equivalent value stored on the authentication service. The value on the authentication service may be identical to the credential provided, it may be a cryptographic hash of the credential, or the service may utilize some other means whereby a proposed value is compared to a known value to determine a match or no-match condition. As such, a symmetric authentication system must maintain a central database of credentials for comparison to validate authentication requests. Some examples of commonly used symmetric authentication include passwords, shared secrets, biometric authentication, and Kerberos authentication.

When authentication is performed using a symmetric authentication system, the actual credential (or a cryptographically symmetrical representation thereof) must be transmitted between the authenticating system and the authentication service. If the authentication service is not on the same machine, the credential becomes subject to theft and reuse if not appropriately protected.

Symmetric credentials are in use everywhere and are ideal for authenticating a human to a computer. The key benefit of symmetric authentication is its ease of use: passwords are easy to remember, a biometric identity is expected to stay the same, and typically encryption and validation speeds of symmetric credentials tend to be faster.

Protection

When transmitted over a network, symmetric credentials must be heavily protected due to their risk of being stolen and reused. Typically, protection of a symmetric credential is achieved through use of encryption and\or an authentication protocol.

Authentication protocols designed to protect symmetric credentials normally utilize some form of hash to ensure confidentiality of the symmetric authenticator. Additionally, a good authentication protocol will also include information about the session (i.e., timestamps, session identifiers, or requested resources) as well as some form of verification to provide assurance that the authentication packet is integral. The goal of these protocols is to provide confidentiality of the symmetric credential being used (the hashing of the credential) as well as non-repudiation (ensuring that the credential is not stolen and replayed, accomplished by including session identifiers, timestamps, etc.).

Encryption is also commonly employed with symmetric authentication to ensure confidentiality during transmission of the credentials. Encryption is effective if the confidentiality of the session can be ensured and the identity of all members involved in the encrypted communication can be assured. For this reason, strong encryption that provides authentication of the hosts involved with the communication and unique session keys is recommended when performing symmetric authentication.

Asymmetric Authentication

In asymmetric authentication, an identity is validated using a pair of mathematically associated keys. In asymmetric cryptography, an algorithm is used to generate a pair of keys whereby any data encrypted by one key in the pair can only be decrypted by the other key in the pair, and not by the key that initially encrypted the data. Typically, one of the keys is kept confidential (referred to as a private key), while the other is distributed widely (the public key) to enable cryptographic communications with any endpoint possessing the private key.

In many cases, this technology is used as part of a service referred to as a public key infrastructure, or PKI. In a PKI, a trusted third party server called a certification authority is used to validate the identity of the asset possessing the private key through cryptographic trust.

For this system to work, the following conditions must be true throughout the validity period of the key pair:

- The algorithm used to generate the key pair must be cryptographically sound such that one key in the pair cannot be used to calculate the opposite key
- The key size must be large enough such that one key cannot be used to deduce the opposite key
- Any keys used to identify an asset within the environment must remain solely in possession of the certified assets
- In a PKI, every certification authority involved in validating the identity of an asset must remain integral and its private key confidential
- In a PKI, the list of certification authorities enlisted to identify assets must remain integral to any host involved in authentication

Asymmetric authentication provides many significant benefits over symmetric authentication. For example, in asymmetric authentication there is no central database of credentials maintained for comparison. This means that credential theft and reuse attacks (such as pass the hash, keylogging, and the like) will not work. If the private key for the identified asset remains confidential, as well as the private keys of any certification authorities involved in authentication, authenticity of the certified asset remains trustworthy.

Additionally, there are special devices designed to allow systems to use the private key's functionality without exposing the key. Smart cards, trusted platform modules (TPM), and hardware security modules (HSM) enable cryptographic operations to be offloaded, thus enabling the use of the private key without exposing the key itself.

Asymmetric authentication also enables multiple keys to be associated with a single identified asset. When used properly, this can add additional context – such as what device the user was using when they authenticated. Additionally, specific keys can be invalidated if compromised without affecting other keys used to authenticate the asset. This capability means that if the private key issued to the TPM of a user's laptop is compromised, only that key needs to be reset: other devices with other keys mapping to that user's identity (such as a smart card or another computer) can remain active and able to be used.

Still another benefit is that assets using asymmetric authentication are not subject to being "compromised by proxy." Think of the passwords that you use to log in to various online services – aren't many of them the same?

This means that compromise of any one of those services may indirectly lead to compromise of the others if the password is stolen. Asymmetric authentication is not subject to this vulnerability because there is no central database of credentials to be exfiltrated.

Unfortunately, asymmetric authentication also has a major drawback. The math involved with asymmetric authentication means that it is not suited for human input. Use of asymmetric authentication relies on humans performing some form of symmetric authentication to a computer and then having the asymmetric authentication performed on their behalf.

The most common form of asymmetric authentication used today is by far SSL, which is the protocol that provides encrypted communication with websites. In SSL, the identity of a remote website (typically based on its domain name) is certified by a certification authority, which is then trusted by the user's computer. Other forms of asymmetric authentication include smart cards, token generators, oAuth, and federated authentication.

Multi-Factor Authentication

Multi-factor authentication is an ideal means of strengthening an authentication design. In multi-factor authentication, more than one form of validation is used to assert the identity of the authenticating entity. Traditionally, authentication is categorized into three different categories:

- Something you know (such as a password)
- Something you have (a card or token)
- Something you are (biometric authentication)

These can be used in combination, such as when a phone is used with a PIN to validate an authentication from another device.

Initial vs. Subsequent Authentication

Adding additional factors to your authentication design strengthens the initial authentication of an entity and is ideal for improving such initial authentication; however, it is typically not suitable for subsequent authentication of users. An important distinction must be made to delineate initial authentication from subsequent authentication.

Initial authentication is the method by which an entity initially identifies itself to a machine – sometimes referred to as the logon process. This is typically a one-time event that occurs when a user begins a session or returns to a previously authenticated session.

Subsequent authentication, by contrast, is authentication of the user to other entities after the initial authentication has occurred. In most cases, these authentication events are likely to be frequent and are therefore unsuitable for multi-factor authentication. Because of this, the operating system is entrusted with the responsibility of performing authentication on the user's behalf. The authentication type will be based on the available protocols, capabilities of the server that the user is authenticating to, and the types of credentials that the user has available.

In short, multi-factor authentication protects the authenticated session, but usually provides no protection to subsequent authentications which happen on the user's behalf by the operating system. Therefore, multi-factor authentication is not an adequate defense if a reusable user credential is stolen. To regain trust in that user's or computer's authentication, all underlying credentials associated with that user or computer must be reset.

Trusted Platform Modules

Machines can act as a factor in multi-factor authentication as well by using devices outside of the control of the operating system. Although many authentication systems rely on the confidentiality of operating system secrets and processes, a machine can perform a type of two-factor authentication when it does not have access to an asymmetric key used for its authentication. For this to work, the operating system must rely on an external device to calculate all authentication on its behalf, such as a trusted platform modules (TPM).

TPMs are devices that manage keys on behalf of the operating system. When these devices are used, the operating system must know a key to the TPM (something it knows), and it must have access to the TPM (something it has). Many of these devices also detect tampering and will not allow the operating system access to its keys until a user provides a previously derived key.

Machine-Specific User Authentication

Historically, credentials have been tied to either the user account or the computer, but rarely both. This was likely in part due to the speed of processors and the computational intensity of asymmetric cryptography. With the advancement of processor technology and the advent of devices such as TPMs, authentication can now be tied to a paired credential which identifies not only the user, but the specific machine he or she is using. This is done by issuing a different key to each device and utilizing a PKI to certify the identity of the user.

Machine-specific user authentication schemes can provide significant benefits when handling incident response scenarios. For example, if a computer becomes infected with malware, all credentials associated with that machine can be eliminated automatically, thus reducing the scope and impact of the compromise. Additionally, the user will not have to perform a password change as his or her credentials on any other machine would remain valid.

Putting it Together

After this discussion on the nuances of authentication system, the question stands – what is the best use of authentication to provide a secure, yet still productive, enterprise? The good news is that the drawbacks of one type of authentication match perfectly with the benefits of another, thus creating a scenario which is ideal for design.

Use Asymmetric Authentication for Externally-Exposed Network Communication

Whenever possible, network authentication which sources from users outside of the service should leverage asymmetric authentication mechanisms. Use of asymmetric authentication enables a strong identity platform which does not have a central key store which can be dumped. A properly implemented asymmetric authentication scheme is not natively susceptible to replay attacks, therefore increasing the trust in the identity platform employed.

It is important to remember that many authentication schemes accept asymmetric authentication to establish a session, but then utilize a static symmetric credential to identify users in subsequent authentication. This is typically a throwback to password-centric authentication schemes and is used for compatibility. If possible, the network authentication system should only support asymmetric credentials for establishing an authenticated session.

Authentication between systems within a service (and over trusted network links) can safely utilize symmetric authentication (such as Kerberos or NTLM) or asymmetric authentication if the service is believed to remain integral. In service-centric architecture, all authentication between systems providing a given service will utilize a private authentication and authorization system, thus reducing the likelihood of stolen asymmetric credentials having authorization within the service. If the service's authentication or authorization systems are compromised, no part of the service can be considered integral anyway.

Store Keys on a TPM or Smart Card

Asymmetric keys need to have the private key available to them for use in user authentication. Storing these keys with the operating system means that there is an inherent risk that the operating system can be manipulated to decrypt and provide the private key, thus compromising the identity platform.

Storing keys on a TPM means that the operating system never gets to know the private keys in a key pair. As a result, although a compromise of the operating system may enable the attacker to authenticate as a user, the private key is never exposed and can only be used from that machine. Eliminate the attacker from the machine and you can be confident that authentication will remain integral.

Utilize Strong Symmetric Authentication to Access TPM Keys

Symmetric authentication is ideal for authenticating users because of its ease of use. Historically, passwords have been leveraged for network authentication due to their simplicity; however, there are numerous conditions where a password can be compromised and used from anywhere (this was the reason we leveraged asymmetric authentication for network communication).

Unlike network authentication, local authentication can leverage symmetric authentication schemes effectively since credentials used for authentication are only valid locally. This means that if your password were exposed in a website breach, the hackers would still need some way to find your computer and have an interface where they can utilize password authentication over a network, which doesn't need to exist.

To further improve this scenario, it is necessary to use some form of non-password symmetric authentication (such as biometric) so that there is no ability to use a password whatsoever. This addition to the authentication scheme will make network-based credential theft attacks nearly impossible.

An additional benefit of using local authentication is that user passwords no longer need to be rotated. This design effectively reduces the risks associated with a password-based authentication scheme since a password cannot be used for network authentication. To compromise this system, the hacker now needs two factors – the machine (something you have) and the password (something you know) – which brings us to our next concept.

Implement Machine-Specific User Authentication

The next step in the equation is handling incidents on the network. Asymmetric credentials are typically issued for extended periods of time (commonly years) due to their strength. This extended validity period can become problematic when dealing with an incident response scenario, especially if a single asymmetric credential is held by multiple devices.

Use of machine-specific credentials provides significant control to administrators, allowing them to invalidate

- A single compromised user on a single device, in the event of a compromised user profile
- All users on a single device, in the case of a compromised machine

- A compromised credential for a single user, in the case of a compromised credential mapped to the user account
- A single user throughout the enterprise, in the case of termination or a backdoor account

Machine-specific credentials also simplify the user's authentication process: passwords can be replaced by PINs or biometric authentication with no implication for network authentication strength.

A Case for the Cloud

A common topic today is the concept of cloud migration and its impact on information security. The topic of cloud security is a tough, multi-faceted decision involving not only technical implications and risks, but also legal, compliance, and a myriad of other concerns.

In this chapter, we will discuss what it means to migrate workloads to a cloud service provider from a risk perspective and discuss the associated benefits and risks.

Cloud services can be broken into three distinct categories, each with their own risks and benefits:

- Software as a Service (SaaS)
- Platform as a Service (PaaS)
- Infrastructure as a Service (IaaS)

Transitive Vulnerability

One concern with any cloud service provider is the potential for transitive vulnerability – a condition whereby compromise of a cloud service provider's infrastructure can lead to compromise of a customer's service hosted on that infrastructure. This situation manifests when a cloud service provider becomes compromised by a targeted attacker, thus potentially breaching the confidentiality and\or integrity of any services hosted by that provider. An adept attacker can leverage this condition to gain authorization in a target's enterprise if the hosted service owns or maintains credentials which provide authorization to services hosted in the customer's on-premises environment or to other cloud services potentially hosted by other providers.

Any credentials owned or maintained by services hosted within cloud service providers should be monitored for anomalous activity. Given the nature of cloud services, activity performed by these accounts should be very consistent. As such, they are likely well-suited for anomaly-based monitoring. Where possible, cloud services are an ideal location for demarcation of authorization, perhaps through a separate domain infrastructure or through complete credential isolation.

Service Administration Accounts

Another area of significant concern surrounds accounts used to manage the cloud service and its integration with other services. These accounts can circumvent security controls and provide access to resources hosted by the cloud service provider, thus potentially bypassing normal detection. Any use of these accounts should be closely monitored.

Risks associated with service administration accounts may include the ability to edit or replace virtual hard drive files; to grant access to confidential data (i.e., mailboxes or other protected data); to intercept, monitor, or re-route network traffic of interest; and to edit or manipulate hosted applications which could lead to covert channels, credential theft, or obscure persistence (i.e. webshell or Trojan implant).

Software as a Service (SaaS)

Software as a Service (SaaS) is a category of applications which are completely hosted by an external organization. SaaS cloud services are ideal for several reasons, in part because they are a fully outsourced capability. SaaS is typically only lightly integrated with their customer environment, which provides ideal isolation from a targeted attack perspective. Additionally, SaaS solutions tend to scale very well, and that scalability becomes the responsibility of the SaaS provider. Also, some SaaS providers take on the burden associated with operating in regulated industries on the customer's behalf, thus transferring the liability contractually and saving money and effort on their customer's part. With no need for a datacenter or support staff, many organizations gravitate towards SaaS solutions. But what does this mean for information security?

Whereas SaaS services provide little risk of transitive vulnerability, they do run the risk of compromising the confidentiality or integrity of the data they host. In other words, if the SaaS provider becomes compromised, any information that an organization houses may be compromised as well. Using a SaaS service means that a significant amount of trust is placed in the processes used within the provider's operations.

Another potential concern resides with integration of a SaaS solution with other on-premises services. SaaS services may require credentials and authorization above that of a standard user to enable their integration into your environment. Service accounts provided for use with a SaaS service should be given explicit authorization and be closely monitored to ensure that the account performs only the activities it needs for integration. Attempts for the account to perform other activities may be an indication of a potential compromise of the SaaS service provider.

Additionally, it may be prudent to ensure that the provider is certified by a third-party certification body, such as the Cloud Security Alliance, the

MSP Alliance, or the National Institute of Standards and Technology. Organizations meeting third-party industry certification are more likely to utilize safe data handling and operating procedures, thus increasing their trustworthiness. It is worth noting that this certification should be standard for all cloud service offerings hosting any form of critical data.

Finally, it is important to ensure that the breach notification process is formally documented in the contract and is sufficient for the organization. If a cloud service provider is breached, any data they host may be at risk of compromise. The organization should ensure that the cloud provider provides guaranteed notification of any security breach that may involve their data.

Additionally, organizations may consider taking a multi-factor approach to data stored in a cloud service where possible using cryptography. For example, if the organization's SaaS service hosts sensitive documents, they might consider using document encryption (ideally, rights management) to ensure that in the event of a breach the attacker remains unable to read sensitive information. Ideally, this encryption service would be hosted by a different provider or in-house.

Platform as a Service (PaaS)

In a platform as a service (PaaS), a provider offers a hosted environment that allows the customer to develop custom services. PaaS is like having a common runtime environment in the cloud, whereby the service provider maintains the underlying operating system and the customer remains responsible for anything deployed on it.

Managing risk in a PaaS environment means monitoring alerts raised by the service provider as well as any security events generated by the application hosted on the PaaS environment. Developers involved in creation of a PaaS-hosted application should understand and follow software development lifecycle (SDLC) procedures to ensure durability against attack. Additionally, it is important to log and monitor unhandled exception conditions to identify potential attempts to exploit vulnerable code.

PaaS providers should provide a service level for disclosure of any attacks against their infrastructure which may impact the hosted organization in any way. Compromise of the underlying PaaS infrastructure may subsequently expose guest tenants to potential breach of confidentiality or integrity. Additionally, it is necessary to ensure that the hosting organization employs a capable information security team to detect and respond to the presence of targeted attackers within the infrastructure – inability to detect targeted attacker presence can be just as bad as (or worse than) a poor reporting service level agreement. If possible, third party attestation of these practices is ideal.

Infrastructure as a Service (IaaS)

An IaaS hosting service essentially supplies the hardware and networking infrastructure, while you bring your own operating system and applications. IaaS is essentially a hosted virtual machine and can be ideal for disaster recovery of on-site workloads or for expanding capacity without expanding your datacenter footprint.

In IaaS, transitive vulnerability can be a major concern since security of your systems can be directly impacted by security practices of the organization. For example, if a hosting provider's infrastructure is compromised, the attacker may gain access to your hosted virtual machines through the compromised host and gain authorization by virtue that they can mount disks used by the VM for editing.

The most likely attacks that would manifest from a compromised IaaS provider would be exfiltrating sensitive data from the VM, adding an executable to run when the VM powers up, or reconfiguring a VM to host a new service specifically for malicious purposes (such as adding a SSH server that dials out to the attacker during boot). As such, defenses should focus on ensuring VM integrity and confidentiality.

One way to protect virtual disks from data theft or manipulation is by employing drive-level encryption. Technologies such as Microsoft's BitLocker makes malicious manipulation of a virtual hard drive significantly more difficult. Additionally, this technology prevents reading of sensitive data by an attacker who does not have access to the associated key. Where possible, keys for the BitLocker drives should be stored in a hardware security module (HSM) to prevent theft.

Another possibility is to add third party health attestation to your application's start-up process. For example, files and configurations that are part of the system boot process can be sent to a central service for alerting and monitoring. The third-party service may be hosted on-premises or by a different IaaS provider to ensure compromise of one provider does not permit an attacker to tamper with the attestation service.

Lastly, it is important to limit the authorization that the hosted services have with other critical services to reduce the impact in the event of compromise. A compromised VM will provide system-level authorization to the attacker; therefore, anything processed by the VM can be tampered with or stolen.

Epilogue

Cybersecurity and targeted attack is an advanced and evolving field bringing light to our previously lax approach to systems design. The intent of this book has been to highlight the importance of proper systems design and to enable the reader to think about the various potential abuse cases which manifest in poor authentication and authorization design.

Hackers typically do not worry about how a system *should* be used, but rather focus on how that system *can* be used to their benefit. While many news articles and blog posts highlight specific tools and attacks that different attackers utilize, usually what is being abused is the core design principals of access and authorization.

Although concepts such as "bring your own device" architecture may limit visibility, they can improve user experience and provide credential isolation if implemented properly. While cloud computing may cause concern for some IT professionals, proper design can improve security, limit overhead costs, and enable an organization to dynamically scale well beyond an in-house maintained infrastructure.

As long as there is crime there will be criminals, and as long as your organization has either intellectual property or money there will be hackers interested in stealing it. Some high-profile organizations are likely to be under constant attack from the most advanced determined human adversaries, thus making cybersecurity a necessary part of their decision-making process. Organizations employing information security professionals who are able to think like a hacker are undoubtedly more likely to stand strong against attacks, whereas others will make news headlines due to data breaches, credit card theft, ransom, and destruction.

One notable attribute of hackers is their passion to learn, mentor, and experiment. This book represents years of work, but contains only a portion of what an effective cybersecurity professional should understand. To excel in cybersecurity it is important to learn continuously; thus, my best recommendation is to find those wiser and become their mentee, attend the various hacker conferences and see the latest in targeted attack, download hacking tools into a lab and learn how they work, and when designing security, always remember to think like a hacker.

Acknowledgements

Although this book may be short, it was not without a significant amount of help from my friends, family, and colleagues.

First, I would like to thank my wife who has put up with the amount of time I dedicated to this book, which in many cases was in addition to my already grueling schedule. Without you, I would never have had the inspiration, drive, and passion that led me to create something great.

Additionally, I would like to thank a few of my mentors, namely Bill Mosley, Nate Bahta, Robert Ashe, Scott Becker, IB Terry, Chris Ard, and Elik Diaz who helped me learn how to establish myself and grow in this ever-changing field. I sincerely believe that I could not be where I am today without your assistance and advice throughout my career.

I owe great gratitude to my various colleagues who reviewed my work and helped ensure that its content was relevant, accurate, and useful to the field. Mark Simos, Chris Ard, and Chris Kirk, your inputs were infinitely valuable in shaping the content and tone of this book – your review of my drafts proved invaluable in assembling the final product.

In addition, I would like to thank my professional editors, Dr. Shannon Zinck and Dr. Michael Shuman, for your review of my manuscript. Your review helped me reach the polished final draft that I sought for my finished product. I also owe great thanks to my friends Dr. Phil Sipiora and Austin Sipiora for putting me in touch with these very skilled professionals and helping me understand the publishing process.

I would like to thank John Hines for helping put me in touch with some of the various publishers considered for this book. These connections will most definitely help in distributing future releases of this book as well as hopefully others.

I would also like to thank the Ghostbusters, Scott, Special K, IB, Beard, Captain, Jailbird, Sultan, Crystal Crawfish, Jeremiah, and the rest of our team, for providing me the opportunity to learn just about everything I know in the realm of targeted attack and malware. Much of the knowledge in this book is the result of many lessons learned and long hours of research we performed in support of our customers.

About the Author

Michael Melone is a Principal Cybersecurity Consultant specializing in targeted attack and determined human adversaries for Microsoft's Global Incident Response and Recovery (GIRR) team with over 17 years of experience in information security. Michael is an honor graduate of Capella University holding a master's degree in IT management specializing in  information assurance and security. Additionally, he holds a number of industry certifications, including being a 10 year holder of the (ISC)^2 CISSP certification.

Website: http://www.PersistentAdversary.com

LinkedIn: http://www.LinkedIn.com/in/mjmelone

Twitter: @PowerShellPoet

13263908R00059

Printed in Germany
by Amazon Distribution
GmbH, Leipzig